living in
financial
victory

tony evans

MOODY PUBLISHERS

CHICAGO

All Scripture quotations are taken from the *New American Standard Bible®*,
Copyright © 1960, 1962, 1963, 1968, 1971, 1972, 1973, 1975, 1977, 1995
by The Lockman Foundation. Used by permission. (www.Lockman.org)

Editor: Kathryn Hall
Interior Design: Ragont Design
Cover Design: Barb Fisher / LeVan Fisher Design
Cover Image:Colin Anderson / Getty Images

ISBN 978-0-8024-0723-8

We hope you enjoy this book from Moody Publishers. Our goal is to provide high-quality, thought-provoking books and products that connect
truth to your real needs and challenges. For more information on other
books and products written and produced from a biblical perspective, go
to www.moodypublishers.com or write to:

Moody Publishers
820 N. LaSalle Boulevard
Chicago, IL 60610

Moody Publishers is committed to caring wisely for God's creation
and uses recycled paper whenever possible. The paper in this book
consists of 10 percent post-consumer waste.

1 3 5 7 9 10 8 6 4 2

Printed in the United States of America

CONTENTS

STEWARDSHIP

During the time I was a student at Dallas Seminary, my wife and I used to house-sit for people in an exclusive area of Dallas. These homes were something else; a real contrast to our tiny, cramped apartment.

For every assignment, our job was to watch over the house, keep things going, and keep it clean. In exchange, we got to live like royalty in another kingdom for a few days. The home's owners would stock the refrigerator and pay us for staying there while they went away on business or vacation.

The families usually gave us the run of the place. But even though there was great opportunity for enjoyment, there were also definite limitations on that enjoyment. Each family had rules they wanted us to follow while they were away. And we agreed to follow the rules because it was not our home. Yet sometimes I used to tell the guys at the seminary, "Come over to my pad this afternoon. You have to check this place out."

You see, I wanted to fully maximize the situation. For a brief time I wanted to act like I owned the home; that it was mine to do what I pleased. But my wife was always careful to remind me, "People shouldn't come over, Tony."

I would say, "Why?"

Her response was, "Because this is not our house."

She was reminding me that we did not own the house. We had to be careful about what we did because the owners were only letting us use their property. My wife was wise to point out that we were managers over what someone else owned.

Friend, here's my point. In this life, none of what you think you own do you really own. All that you so call "own" really belongs to God. What Satan wants to do is make you think you can do whatever you want with it, independently of God. But that is definitely not so.

In my example of this principle, every home we watched while I was in seminary was the kingdom of the family who owned it. As temporary managers, we were merely the stewards of the home. It belonged to someone else and, therefore, we had to function according to their agenda—not ours.

Our job was simply to manage someone else's property that had been entrusted to our care. In a similar way, a key element in carrying out God's kingdom agenda is our management of what He has given to us. This is the biblical definition of stewardship. In God's eyes, it is an extremely important job. As a result, we need to learn how to be good stewards, or managers, of what has been entrusted to us.

GOOD STEWARDSHIP UNLOCKS THE DOOR

In a more formal definition of stewardship, it is described as *the process of protecting and expanding the assets and resources of another.* I am here to tell you that it is only through following the biblical principles of stewardship that you will attain a life of financial victory. If you choose to view your finances apart from God's ownership, you will fail to actualize the financial blessings that He has tied to His precepts. In fact, not only will you fail to actualize the blessings, you will also suffer loss.

THE COVENANT AND STEWARDSHIP

The story has been told about a son who wanted to give his father a thank-you gift on Father's Day. The young man desired to let his dad know how much he loved and valued him. So the son went out and found the most exotic gift he could find: a talking parakeet. This parakeet spoke five languages and could stand on one leg while singing "The Yellow Rose of Texas." It was an amazing bird.

The day after Father's Day, the son called his dad to

see how he liked his gift. He asked the older gentleman, "How did you like the parakeet, Dad?"

His father replied, "It was delicious, thank you."

Obviously, the father missed the point of the gift.

Many of us in Christian circles today have missed the point of God's gift of money. While we may recognize that He has given it to us, we do not fully realize its purpose. Far too often we spend it, consume it, or waste it—rather than maximizing it to its fullest potential.

The truth is, God has a purpose when it comes to your finances. An excellent summary statement of the purpose God has for money is found in the book of Deuteronomy, where we read,

> But you shall remember the Lord your God, for it is He who is giving you power to make wealth, *that He may confirm His covenant* which He swore to your fathers, as it is this day. (8:18, emphasis mine)

Here we see God's main reason for affording His people with the power to make wealth. It is to "confirm His covenant" with the people of God. Now, keep in mind, this doesn't mean that everyone will be "wealthy" by the world's standards. God is not your cosmic slot machine. In the preceding verses of chapter 8, wealth is defined as having enough to eat, a place to live, herds, flocks, and enough to be sufficiently satisfied.

Generally, when we talk about the "wealthy" in America, we are referring to the megawealthy: those who are millionaires and above. However, when God talks about the wealthy in Scripture, He is referring to those having enough in *all* areas of life, along with their ability to enjoy it.

What, then, is the covenant we are talking about? The covenant is God's kingdom program. In order to understand the covenant, we need to first understand the kingdom. The kingdom, simply put, refers to *the theocratic operation and implementation of the rule of God over every part of creation.* Furthermore, the kingdom has an agenda, which is *the visible demonstration of the comprehensive rule of God over every area of life.*

Within this framework, the kingdom is not so much a reference to a location as it is a divine source. It points to heaven's presence and operation in history. For believers, submission to God's kingdom agenda opens up the flow of heaven's involvement in our lives on earth.

There are four aspects of every kingdom. First, a kingdom must have a king, or a ruler. In the kingdom of heaven, God is the King. A kingdom also must have subjects of the kingdom, those in subjection to the ruler. We are God's subjects. A kingdom also has rules, which the ruler oversees. In God's kingdom, the rules are biblical principles and truths.

Finally, a kingdom also has a realm: a scope over which the king rules. David tells us in the book of Psalms, "The earth is the Lord's, and all it contains, the world, and those who dwell in it" (Psalm 24:1). The whole world is God's kingdom.

With God as the Ruler, if we are to abide in His kingdom and receive the blessings and the benefits therein, we must follow the biblical precepts and regulations given to us in Scripture. The Word of God provides a road map and contains everything we need to know in order to enjoy success in our personal lives, including success in our finances.

Now here is the principle of the covenant: God expands His kingdom program in history through His subjects, the body of Christ. When God can trust His subjects to act as good stewards by receiving His blessings and provision and using them to advance His kingdom, He is motivated to give more.

From Genesis to Revelation you will see this word and concept called the covenant. Ultimately, God's covenant is intended to bless the person in the covenant in order for that person to be a blessing to others. For example, in the covenant God gave to Abraham, He said, "I will bless you, and make your name great; and so you shall be a blessing" (Genesis 12:2).

The covenantal principles of blessing carry through to the new covenant He has given us as well. Jesus, the author and mediator of the new covenant, shares those blessings as His people meet with Him in communion (see 1 Corinthians 10:16–17).

In consideration of God's purpose for establishing His covenant with you, examine your innermost thoughts. If you are only thinking about your house, your job, your car, your clothes, and your money, then you are thinking outside of the covenant. You are limiting what God can and will do through you in order to bless you because you are not thinking with a covenant mindset. You are thinking about *your* kingdom rather than about God's kingdom.

Victory through the Covenant

God is interested in His kingdom building program. As His stewards, He wants us to achieve the highest level of success in doing our part. Since the covenant is the driving word within God's kingdom, understanding and living out the covenant is the key to your spiritual and financial victory. Let's delve deeper, using this analogy.

> ## God's provisions, promises, and His will flows through His covenant.

If you are like me, a citizen of the United States of America, you live underneath a covenantal document called the Constitution. The Constitution is the umbrella document under which the "kingdom" of the USA operates. This unique document outlines many rules and regulations, including many freedoms, for the citizens who live within its realm of influence.

In fact, you may regularly hear people say, "I know

my rights," when they feel that they have been unjustly treated. They are appealing to their constitutional rights under the kingdom called America.

Furthermore, if you are a Christian, then you are also part of another kingdom. You are a part of God's kingdom, along with its covenantal rights. However, if you do not know your rights then you won't know how to exercise them. You will not know how best to maximize the rights and privileges granted to you as a citizen of God's kingdom.

In the Bible, a covenant is an agreement similar to a contract. A contract is a legal and officially binding agreement. When people enter into a contract, they become contractually obligated by the terms within the agreement. A covenant, however, goes beyond a contract because it also assumes a relationship. While it contains a legal and officially binding agreement, it also includes a relational aspect that a contract is not required to have. Such is the case with marriage, which is a relational covenantal agreement drawn up between a man and a woman.

The reason why you need to understand your covenantal rights and privileges is so you will know how to live a victorious life with kingdom authority. God's provisions, promises, and His will flow through His covenant. If you don't know the agreement you are operating within, you won't know how to benefit from it. You will not know how to exercise the legal authority that is yours to carry out, provided you function within the terms of the covenant.

Just prior to giving Israel the Ten Commandments,

God told them something very important related to His covenant. He said,

> Now then, if you will indeed obey My voice and keep My covenant, then you shall be My own possession among all the peoples, for all the earth is Mine; and you shall be to Me a kingdom of priests and a holy nation. (Exodus 19:5–6)

God told Moses to tell the Israelites that if they would keep His covenant, He would make them uniquely blessed out of all the nations. As a result of Israel's obedience, they would be entitled to certain privileges, protections, and even honor.

Unfortunately, we live in a day where people misunderstand the concept of God's covenant. Somehow we miss the fact that He wants us to take the resources we are given and be fruitful and multiply them so that others will be brought into the kingdom. As a result, we fail to realize that the covenant is about the advancement of God's kingdom.

You can be a Christian all day long and be on your way to heaven yet never experience the benefits of being underneath the covenant. Financial victory only comes when you conform to God's precepts which He has set forth in His Word. Covenantal positioning is the key to partaking in kingdom privilege, authority, and victory.

PROSPERING GOD'S WAY

There is no way around it—you can't experience the prosperity of the covenant without first exemplifying a commitment to the covenant. In no uncertain terms, God's blessings are always tied to keeping His covenant. Scripture tells us what we can expect when we obey this command, "So keep the words of this covenant to do them, *that* you may prosper in all that you do" (Deuteronomy 29:9, emphasis mine).

Here we find evidence straight from God's Word: you will prosper when you keep God's covenant. However, also know that your level of prosperity in the new covenant is directly tied to the level of your spiritual development.

Let me explain. One of the greatest secrets about the covenant that I could ever tell you is that the covenant is designed to produce progress in your life. As you operate in agreement with the covenant of God, you get the flow of God's power, position, provision, and authority.

One of the problems that we are experiencing financially in the body of Christ is an unfortunate disconnect between the spiritual aspects of the covenant and the material aspects of the tangible world in which we live. As a believer, you are never to separate God's covenantal purposes, the spiritual part of your life, from your material, physical life.

In biblical theology, the two are always connected. When John wrote his third epistle, he opened with the following, "Beloved, I pray that in all respects you may prosper and be in good health, just as your soul prospers" (3 John 1:2). The apostle was not only praying for believers' material prosperity but also physical and spiritual prosperity. They are all interrelated.

When people live without that connection, they frequently wind up in unsatisfactory situations. Those who make a lot of money yet neglect the spiritual component and purpose of wealth often live with empty souls and broken lives. They only use their money in an attempt to camouflage the emptiness within. This is sometimes known as prosperity theology, which often seeks to emphasize the material above the spiritual.

On the opposite end of the Christian spectrum are those who live with a poverty mentality. In the name of being spiritual, they only wind up being unproductive and failing to contribute to their own needs as well as to the needs of the body of Christ and the advancement of His kingdom. What these individuals misunderstand is that God is not opposed to wealth. He is opposed to the wrong use and motivation for it.

However, let me emphasize this fact as well. There are plenty of unbelievers who are living without a connection to God yet they experience financial gain. They just don't experience the blessings of God in that gain. In fact, a lot of people who have a lot of money are more miserable now with an abundance of wealth than they ever were without it. A blessing is not merely the increase. The blessing is in the ability to enjoy and extend what you have been given (see Proverbs 10:22; Acts 20:35).

Another important characteristic about the covenant that many people do not understand is that the covenant contains a vital covering that Jesus provided for us when He finished His work on the Cross (see Matthew 26:28; 1 Corinthians 11:3). If you are operating underneath the covenant and in line with God's covenantal precepts, you are operating underneath His covering. This is what enables you to prosper the way God intends.

The covering God offers is similar to an umbrella. If you are outside and it begins to rain, you open up an umbrella. That is, if you are so fortunate to have one with you. The umbrella doesn't stop the rain, but it does stop the rain from raining on you. In other words, when you are covered by the umbrella, it does not change the circumstances around you, but it will change what is allowed to directly affect you.

Sadly, many people are operating financially uncovered. They are suffering in debt, not being able to enjoy the money that they do have. The reason why so many people's finances are so messed up is because they are not covered through alignment under the covenant. They are not fully satisfied simply due to the fact that they are not honoring God's covenant. Therefore, when the rains of life come—and they will—these unfortunate ones will have no covering.

As Christians, it is highly essential to know that the covenant exists and is designed to provide a way for God's people to prosper. Yet, also be aware that when you live life uncovered and not in alignment with the covenant, you will experience the resultant effects of functioning apart from the King and His kingdom covering.

We are suffering financially in our personal lives, families, churches, and as a nation simply because we are not operating according to the rules and precepts of the covenant. Realignment must take place in order for our financial lives to recover and be in order. Just as you must be under an umbrella for the umbrella to benefit you, likewise, you must be under God's covenant for the covenant to cover and prosper you.

But there is always hope for those who have been operating outside of God's covering. As the people of God, we can rejoice in the truth that we can repent and turn back to Him. Because He assures us of His covering, we never have to be like the evil, who prosper outside of God's protection (see Psalm 73:12). Scripture warns us that they do so with a hole in their soul. God confirms His covenant with His people, but these unfortunate ones are set on a slippery slope without the ability to fully enjoy the long-term satisfaction of their gain (v. 18).

At the end of the day, we must come to understand that bearing financial fruit means more than stockpiling money. Those who prosper God's way are able to reach out to others and fully benefit from what God has so freely given.

THE PARABLE OF THE STEWARDS

Jesus taught us the primary precepts for living a life of financial victory through similar parables that are recorded in both the books of Matthew and Luke (Matthew 25; Luke 19). A parable is a story that is laid beside a principle in order to help the listener or reader better understand the principle. The story gives life and reality to the principle that God wants you to learn. It helps you grab, feel, comprehend, and ultimately live out the principle. Jesus regularly taught in parables in order to teach kingdom principles.

As He did so many times, Jesus began His parables on the kingdom with words such as those found in Matthew 25:1, "Then the kingdom of heaven will be comparable to . . ."

With the use of this phrase, notice that Jesus is comparing the kingdom of heaven to some aspect of our earthly lives. Far too many of us are satisfied with the part of Christianity that takes us to heaven. Yet some neglect the part that brings a bit of heaven down to earth. In order to bring to earth what is in heaven, the will of God must be done. His rule must prevail, which is why Jesus took the time to clearly articulate and illustrate God's rule in various areas of our lives.

The parable that we are about to look at deals with the area of stewardship and directly applies to our finances. In Luke 19:11–27, Jesus lays out the standards by which we, being designated God's stewards, are to function on His behalf as part of His kingdom. They are the standards by which our stewardship will be evaluated. Let's unfold this important passage.

A STEWARD IS ENTRUSTED
WITH RESOURCES TO MANAGE

Jesus introduced this parable by telling us about a no-bleman who traveled far. We read,

> A nobleman went to a distant country to receive a kingdom for himself, and then return. And he called ten of his slaves, and gave them ten minas and said to them, "Do business with this until I come back." (Luke 19:12–13)

Now, at closer scrutiny, let's consider the meaning of this passage. In the parable, Christ is the nobleman going away to lay claim to the kingdom He won by virtue of His victory on Calvary. The "distant country" is heaven, from which He will return one day to establish His visible king-dom in the millennium. But in the meantime, King Jesus has given His servants something to manage, and He has commanded us to manage it well until He returns.

THE CLOTHES ON YOUR BACK ARE ONLY THERE BECAUSE GOD MADE THEM POSSIBLE.

From this parable, we see the first principle that stewardship means: God owns it all. The nobleman gave the slaves a portion of money from his coffers. The slaves didn't contribute anything. Here we are being taught that God created it all, so it all belongs to Him (see Revelation 4:11).

Although this principle may be easy enough to state, living as though we understand it is far more challenging. The truth is, God's total ownership is inescapable. He declared it is so in the book of Psalms:

> Every beast of the forest is Mine . . .
> and everything that moves in the field is Mine.
> If I were hungry I would not tell you:
> For the world is Mine, and all it contains.
> (from Psalm 50:10–12)

God is the owner of His kingdom by virtue of the creation. David tells us elsewhere, "The earth is the Lord's, and all it contains, the world, and those who dwell in it" (Psalm 24:1). Friend, God owns it all, including you. The question is quite straightforward: "Do you not know that your body is a temple of the Holy Spirit who is in you, whom you have from God, and that you are not your own?" (1 Corinthians 6:19)

Allow me to explain it this way. Since God owns everything, everything we claim to own is only ours relatively speaking. It is not ours absolutely speaking. The money that you have in your possession right now was printed on paper that was ground from the pulp of trees that grew on God's property. The car that you drive was shaped out of metal whose elements were dug from God's earth. The clothes on your back are only there because God made them possible.

I remember teaching my oldest son, Anthony, about giving. One day, I told him, "Anthony, whatever you get, the first ten percent of everything goes to God. And that's just the minimum." Then I gave him five dollars for an allowance. I knew the question that was going to come next.

"Dad, that rule doesn't apply to my allowance, does it?" I told him that it did.

"So you want me to take fifty cents out of my five dollars and give it to the Lord?"

I knew he wasn't getting the idea, so I proceeded to explain. "Anthony, it works like this. Where did you get the five dollars?"

"You gave it to me."

"Right. And where did I get the five dollars?"

"Well, you got it from your salary as pastor of the church."

"Right again," I replied and continued my explanation. "Your five-dollar allowance came from my salary at the church, which was provided by the offerings of the congregation. Now, where did the people get the money to give so I could be paid and you could have your five dollars? They got it from their salaries at the places where they work."

I was just getting warmed up, as I asked, "Now, Anthony, if the people got the money to give from the places where they work so they could pay me, and you could have your five dollars, then what are the things they need in order to work?"

At that point, we went through the whole list: a car, clothes, a place to live, food for strength, even the air we all breathe. We then traced everything back to God.

"So," I told him. "Since there is nothing we have that didn't come from God, giving Him ten percent is no big deal."

Then I asked him, "Anthony, do you have a problem with giving God fifty cents?"

He said, "No, Dad. I'll give a dollar, I guess."

I think he got the message. My point is, the clearer you see God's hand in everything, the less problem you will have accepting His ownership and honoring that ownership. This is the first step on the path to financial victory.

Job 1:21 acknowledged that we came into this world naked. The only reason we aren't going out naked is because somebody else will dress us that final time. Death is the ultimate reminder that we own nothing. That's why James warns business people not to boast with such statements like, "Today, I'm going here to cut a deal; then tomorrow I'm going there to cut a deal" (4:13–15, my paraphrase). When you study his words, you will find they are a stark reminder of a very critical fact. That is, we don't know whether we'll even be here tomorrow. Our lives are entirely in God's hands.

GOD DOESN'T SHARE OWNERSHIP

Here's the corollary to point one (God owns it all):
God does not share His ownership with anyone.

A very long time ago, there was a being who tried to
share ownership with God. His name was Lucifer, the
chief angel. Lucifer wanted to turn heaven into a joint
venture, desiring to split God's throne with Him fifty-
fifty. But Lucifer got booted out of heaven because God
does not share His ownership with anyone.

Tragically, any attempt you or I make to share ownership with God puts us on the side of Satan. It means we
are operating out of the same attitude of pride.

We'll get back to Luke 19 a little later, but now I want
to show you an important warning from Deuteronomy.
As Israel was about to enter the Promised Land of Canaan,
Moses cautioned the people:

> Beware that you do not forget the Lord your God by
> not keeping His commandments and His ordinances
> and His statutes which I am commanding you today;
> otherwise, when you have eaten and are satisfied, and
> have built good houses and lived in them, and when
> your herds and your flocks multiply, and your silver
> and gold multiply, and all that you have multiplies,
> then your heart will become proud and you will for-
> get the Lord your God who brought you out from the
> land of Egypt, out of the house of slavery. . . Other-
> wise, you may say in your heart, 'My power and the

strength of my hand made me this wealth.' But you shall remember the Lord your God, *for it is He who is giving you power to make wealth*, that He may confirm His covenant which He swore to your fathers, as it is this day. (Deuteronomy 8:11–14, 17–18, emphasis mine)

What a powerful reminder of the very essence of what it means to be a steward. The things we own are really on loan from the Lord. It is God who gives the power to increase our finances. This is the second principle we need to understand about stewardship being the pathway to financial victory: A steward may not own what he has been given, but he is responsible for the management of it.

Do you own your own home? Or do you know someone who owns his or her own home? People will often claim to own their homes when in all actuality they are merely stewards of what the bank owns. If you haven't yet finished paying for the home you say that you own, the bank is the rightful owner of that home. If you don't believe me, just skip a few payments over the next couple of months, and you will discover that I was right. In essence, you are a steward over what someone else owns, and you have been given the responsibility to care for it.

This is similar to what God did with Adam and Eve in the garden. He placed them in the garden and gave them what is known as the *Dominion Covenant*. God said, "Let them rule. . ." (Genesis 1:26). God was still the owner. Adam and Eve were simply positioned as the stewards. They were not given the mandate to rule in order to replace God; rather, they were to manage what God had given them on behalf of Him.

One of the reasons God instituted the tithe was to serve as a reminder to His people that they do not own what He has given to them. In effect, through tithes and offerings, you acknowledge that God owns what He has given you. Giving back to God is a physical act that demonstrates a spiritual reality: God is the owner and you are the steward.

Continuing with the parable in Luke 19, the owner gave each of his ten slaves a mina to operate with. A "mina" was an amount of money worth approximately three to four months' salary for a common laborer in those days. This was a pretty substantial allotment, so these particular servants definitely had something significant to work with.

Please note that each slave got the same amount. Why is that important? Because this parable represents something that all of us have in equal measure. It is what I call our "life potential."

Life potential can be divided into three categories: time, talents, and treasure. Now you may say, "Wait a minute, Tony. I can see where we're all equal in time because everybody has the same twenty-four hours every day to use. But aren't people different in terms of their talents and treasure?"

It's true that people differ in their abilities and resources. But that's not Jesus' point here. The point is the equality of the situation. Each servant had the same

amount of money, and each one had equal opportunity
to do something good with his allotment. God has given
each of us a life potential.

The nobleman's command to his servants, "Do business with this until I come back" (v. 13), gets to the heart
of a steward's responsibility.

The issue is not whether you will accept your stewardship but what you will do with it. The question is: what
kind of business will you do with the Lord's property?

The Greek word for business used here is the word
from which we get the English word *pragmatic*. There's
nothing more pragmatic or practical in life than being a
kingdom steward. Doing business for the King and His
kingdom is using the life potential He has given us to its
fullest.

> ## GOD IS GOING TO MEASURE YOU, NOT YOU AGAINST MR. JONES DOWN THE STREET.

Now let me point out something that will encourage
you in your stewardship. Jesus told this same basic story
a different way in Matthew 25. In the parable of the talents, the three servants were given a different amount of

talents "each according to his own ability" (Matthew 25:15). A talent was a large sum of money.

Since people receive varying resources based on their abilities, in one sense, we don't all have the same amount of time. That is, some people will only live to be forty years old while others will live to be eighty. We don't all have the same amount of money to work with either. And we don't all have the same talents and abilities in the same area.

In summary, the key to the passage in Luke is what we might call "equality of opportunity." The key in Matthew is this: When the King comes back, He will only measure His servants against what He gave them as individuals.

Therefore, no matter how much you may have in terms of resources and abilities, no matter how long you live, the point is that Jesus Christ will not compare you to anyone else. You will only be evaluated against what He gave you.

That's why it is wrong to want what somebody else has. God is going to measure you, not you against Mr. Jones down the street. So if you spend all your time trying to be like the Joneses and never get around to carrying out your stewardship duties, you are going to come up empty-handed when the Owner returns. When Jesus comes back, He is not going to ask you about what He gave your neighbor. He's only going to ask you about what He gave you.

INVESTING WHAT GOD HAS GIVEN YOU

What kind of business does Christ want us to conduct with the resources He has entrusted to us?

In a word, we need to invest, not just spend. Too many of us have accumulated debt that is weighing us down. We spend, spend, spend. So we owe, owe, owe. Yet God wants us to invest what we have been given for the advancement of His kingdom.

Keep this in mind, though. In your efforts to invest wisely, as a steward of God's resources, you are to be content without being passive. God has called you to live a life of contentment. That is, you are to be at ease where you are while simultaneously working diligently and trusting God to enable you to maximize your potential (see Proverbs 30:8; Philippians 4:11–12).

In practical terms, this is what we do in our physical lives. We get an education, attend seminars, or train to become an expert in a certain craft or field. We will expend an enormous amount of energy in order to make a mark for ourselves in this world.

However, if we were to look closely at how much time, energy, and financial investment we make in advancing God's kingdom, our efforts would come up lacking. Far too often, our focus is on our kingdom, our bank account, our house, our car, and our clothes. It is about the advancement of us rather than Him.

If you have children, more than likely they would rather spend than invest any day. We don't have to teach our kids the art of spending. We have to teach them to save. Do you know why kids spend all the time? Simply put, they have a wrong view of the future. Kids spend because the only day they can see is today. Typically, given the chance to get what they want, most teenagers will buy it without worrying about whether they will be broke the next week. Unless they are taught differently, kids don't take investing seriously because they don't take the future seriously.

Let me tell you, this is why the lives of some believers are messed up. They don't seriously believe the Owner is going to come back and ask them what they did with the resources He entrusted to them as His stewards.

Now most of us prepare for the future in other areas. We have insurance policies to cover everything we possess to prepare ourselves for the possibility of future events. In other words, we will do for ourselves what we won't do for God. We plan for what *might* happen by buying insurance. But we fail to plan for what *will* happen— the return of Jesus Christ and the evaluation of our stewardship. In view of that most important event, God wants us to wisely invest the life potential and resources He has given us.

When you consult with a financial planner, he is going to talk to you about what you want to happen twenty, thirty, or even forty years from now. His job is to advise you to save now so that you will have something to live on in the future when you can no longer work. He is going to force your perspective to be future-oriented.

It is the same with the biblical principles of stewardship. These principles also exist to set you up for your retirement. You see, your ultimate retirement will be in
heaven, and it will last a lot longer than your retirement
on earth. Therefore, what you do while here on earth will
play a large part in what you will enjoy and do in heaven.
When you invest in advancing the kingdom on earth,
you are forwarding ahead that which has eternal value at-
tached to it. You are thinking with a future-oriented
mindset. According to Matthew 6:20, you are laying up
for yourself "treasures in heaven, where neither moth nor
rust destroys, and where thieves do not break in or steal."
The bottom line is, what you do now in history to advance God's kingdom will carry over into your retirement
years in His presence. The problem with many Christians
today is that they have become too earthly-minded to be
any heavenly-good. This mindset is counterproductive
both for heaven and for advancing heaven's agenda here
on earth. They have forgotten that "our citizenship is in
heaven" (Philippians 3:20). That is where we will reside
eternally.

To summarize, one day Jesus Christ is going to look
at you and me and say, "Let's see whether the agenda of
My kingdom is better off because of what you did with
what I gave you." He will do so because a steward is responsible to manage the resources of the King. And when
the King returns, the steward will have to give an account
of that responsibility.

EVALUATING A STEWARD

Everybody goes through some version of an annual review at work. Why do companies take the time to hold
this kind of evaluation? Because the boss wants to know
how well his employees have produced. For eight hours a
day, forty hours a week, those employees are on the boss's
time. They are his stewards. They are on his agenda, accepting his money to produce work. A performance review
will give the boss a chance to find out how productive the
employees have been for the company.

A time of evaluation is coming for Jesus Christ's stewards too. Let's pick up His parable in Luke 19:15. "When
[the nobleman] returned, after receiving the kingdom, he
ordered that these slaves, to whom he had given the
money, be called to him in order that he might know
what business they had done."

The nobleman's return is a reference to the coming of
Christ, when He will call His people to account for their
stewardship. Then the issue will be, "How did My company, My kingdom, benefit by what I provided to you?"

Now, a lot of us will be able to show how God's gifts
benefited us. But that's not the question. The issue with a
steward is: how did the King's business fare under your management? Is the King better off? Was His agenda furthered?

The Bible calls this day of evaluation for kingdom
stewards "the judgment seat of Christ." It is described in
two key passages.

The first of these important passages is found in

1 Corinthians, chapter 3. I want to quote it in its entirety
because it is so crucial:

> According to the grace of God which was given to
> me, like a wise master builder I laid a foundation, and
> another is building on it. But each man must be care-
> ful how he builds on it. For no man can lay a founda-
> tion other than the one which is laid, which is Jesus
> Christ. Now if any man builds on the foundation with
> gold, silver, precious stones, wood, hay, straw, each
> man's work will become evident; for the day will show
> it because it is to be revealed with fire, and the fire it-
> self will test the quality of each man's work. If any
> man's work which he has built on it remains, he will
> receive a reward. If any man's work is burned up, he
> will suffer loss; but he himself will be saved, yet so as
> through fire (vv. 10–15).

This passage clearly states that we must be careful
about the kind of building we construct on the foundation
God gives us. In effect, Paul is explaining the outcome of
our stewardship. It is a sober warning that we must be at-
tentive to how we carry out our management of the
money that God gives us. The reason is that our stewardship will be tested one day, and it will have to withstand the fire of Christ's judgment on "that day."

Paul's reference is to the day when Christ will judge
His people—not for salvation—but for rewards based on
our work as stewards. This particular day is described in

2 Corinthians 5:10–11a: "For we must all appear before the judgment seat of Christ, so that each one may be recompensed for his deeds in the body, according to what he has done, whether good or bad. Therefore, knowing the fear of the Lord, we persuade men."

Paul said there is a fiery judgment coming. On the day of evaluation, the fire of Jesus Christ "will test the quality of each man's work" (1 Corinthians 3:13). Hebrews 10:30 also confirms that God will judge His people.

When Jesus comes back, He will come to settle the accounts of those who were on earth. He will want to find out what you did with what He gave you and how it benefited Him and His kingdom. He won't be looking to see or discuss what you did that benefited you. He will be interested in knowing how you advanced His kingdom of heaven in history.

When you lose sight of the return of the Master, and you lose sight that one day you will have a conversation with Him to talk about how you invested the resources put at your disposal, you have lost sight of everything that means anything at all.

Last year, my wife and I were able to take a few days away from the ministry and go on a trip to Corinth. It was truly exciting to see the excavation of a historical city that existed so long ago.

In the excavations, we came across what is known as the Bema seat. This is the judgment seat that Paul referenced in his message to the Corinthians. In Corinthian culture, the Bema seat was the place where

judges convened to rule on court cases or to judge ath-
letic competitions. It was the location where those who
won received honor and recognition, while those who
lost had to stand by and witness the adulation given to
those who had done well.

When Jesus Christ comes back to unite His bride, the
church, with Himself, each of us will stand at the Bema.
There we will be judged based on what we did for Him
and His kingdom. It is not the place where salvation is
granted or decided. Those standing will be saved already.
But it is the place where we will either receive a reward for
what we did for eternity or suffer loss for that which we
mismanaged.

You see, at His judgment seat, Jesus Christ is going
to evaluate how well we invested our resources for Him
and His glory. He will examine the quality of our work.

Many people will give their boss top-quality work
when they go into the office. They won't be late and they
won't do sloppy work. Why? Because their paycheck is
in the boss's pocket. They fear not getting a raise. They
fear not being promoted.

If people will do that for an earthly boss, what should
we do for Jesus Christ? Let me ask you: are you giving
God's kingdom a quality return on the resources He has
blessed you with? Or is God getting leftovers?

Many Christians "tip" God. By the way they live and
use their finances, they say, "God, whatever is left over of
my money, I'll give to You. After I have spent my money
on what I want, then I'll give You something. After I have

used my resources to build my business, You'll get some of it during my retirement years."

Anyone who has that attitude had better read 2 Corinthians 5:11 again. Paul called the judgment seat of Christ a thing that should cause us to fear, or be in awe. This will be a serious judgment.

The reason is that when you are dealing with something expensive, you want it done right. When something is just thrown together, it shows a lack of care. For instance, if you are building an expensive house and the bricks aren't laid right, you are going to get that corrected. Or, let somebody even look like he's going to ding the door of your expensive car. You flip out. You won't even park it beside other cars where it could possibly get dinged. The point is, the more something costs—the more serious you are going to be about it.

God paid a high price for you and me. We cost Him the precious life of His Son. Moreover, He has entrusted us with the stewardship of His kingdom on earth. He has given us the priceless privilege of ruling with Him.

Are we going to turn around and give God sloppy work; namely, our leftover resources?

Are we going to spend thousands of dollars on our houses and cars and clothes and then toss a little tip toward God?

No, God says all of this cost Him too much to let us get away with shoddy stewardship. We are going to be evaluated.

The Bible teaches us this critical lesson. Whatever

you have been given, make sure you give God His portion first. Be sure to honor Jesus Christ so that, according to Colossians 1:18, "He Himself will come to have first place in everything."

The issue of stewardship is not perfection. It is an issue of pattern. Where does God fit in the pattern of how you use your money? Is He first, second, third, or a distant eighth? Is He even thought of at all? God wants your pattern to be that of using His resources to promote His kingdom of heaven on earth. When you put Him first, you will surely reap the rewards of His favor.

REWARDS

Once we understand what stewardship is, what our responsibilities are, and the fact that we will be tested, we are ready to talk about the rewards of stewardship.

You need not shy away from the word reward. Sometimes Christians view the attachment of a reward as something that is less than honorable. While it is certainly less honorable if that is your only reason for serving God, it is not less honorable if it is simply *a* reason for doing it.

First and foremost, out of your love for Him, God wants you to be a good steward and manage what He has given to you. But He has also promised to respond to your honoring of Him with that which is called a reward. Let me remind you of what Paul wrote concerning rewards. In his first letter to the church at Corinth, he stated,

Now if any man builds on the foundation with gold, silver, precious stones, wood, hay, straw, each man's work will become evident; for the day will show it because it is to be revealed with fire, and the fire itself will test the quality of each man's work. If any man's work which he has built on it remains, he will receive a reward. If any man's work is burned up, he will suffer loss; but he himself will be saved, yet so as through fire. (1 Corinthians 3:12–15)

Rewards are such an integral part of our Christian life that Jesus Himself punctuates the very last chapter of the Bible, the last portion of inspired revelation, with a clear announcement concerning them. He says, "Behold, I am coming quickly, and My reward is with Me, to render to every man according to what he has done" (Revelation 22:12). Therefore, if the concept of rewards in a believer's life is not

> WHEN YOU SACRIFICE FOR HIM
> AND GIVE TO HIS KINGDOM,
> THE LORD DOES NOT FORGET IT.

spiritual, then Jesus is not spiritual because He plainly stated that He will be returning to hand out rewards.

There are eternal rewards that you will receive for

biblical stewardship; but there are also temporal rewards that will make life more enjoyable here on earth. One of them is the ability to avoid being enslaved to debt. When you live according to God's principles on money, when you commit to God and sacrifice anything for Him—He will not be your debtor. He will pay up. Not only does God reward in eternity those who give to Him; faithful givers will also reap rewards in the here and now. Jesus declared it to be so;

> Truly I say to you, there is no one who has left house or brothers or sisters or mother or father or children or farms, for My sake and for the gospel's sake, but that he will receive a hundred times as much *now in the present age*, houses and brothers and sisters and mothers and children and farms, along with persecutions; and in the age to come, eternal life. (Mark 10:29–30, emphasis mine)

When you sacrifice for Him and give to His kingdom, the Lord does not forget it. In both the present age and in the age to come, you will be rewarded. Friend, you can never out-give God. I challenge you to try it. You can't. His Word is clear: what you give up for Him, He will return, plus more.

THE FAITHFUL STEWARD

To look at what Scripture says regarding the rewards of stewardship, we need to return again to the parable of

Luke 19. The nobleman has returned from his journey, and he's ready to call his servants in to account for how they used their minas.

The first servant came and said, "Master, your mina has made ten minas more" (v. 16). That's a 1,000 percent increase! This man obviously invested his master's money well. He was able to report, "Master, I took what you gave me and invested it. Look at what I have for you."

What does the Master, who is God, say to this man after he used what he had been given so effectively for the kingdom? He received a threefold reward. The first reward is public recognition; it is the master's public announcement, "Well done" (v.17). When you show up at His judgment seat, there will be nothing like hearing Jesus say, "Well done!" He is going to say it publicly.

Friend, you may be hidden away right now in your work or in your home, but if you do what God has called you to do faithfully and consistently, you will be honored before all of heaven on that day.

I was talking to a close relative who has made a tremendous amount of personal sacrifice in order to serve God fully. I asked her why she had committed so much of her life and resources to Him. Her answer was simply, "Because of that day." Immediately, I knew what she meant. But she continued, "I do everything in light of the day when I will stand before Jesus Christ. I want to hear Him say 'Well done.'"

The second reward this faithful steward received was a kingdom inheritance. The master said, "Because you have been faithful in a very little thing, you are to be in authority over ten cities" (v.17).

Most people have a wrong view of the kingdom. Throughout eternity, we will not be floating around on clouds singing songs and playing harps. In addition to worshiping God in heaven, we will have a great deal to do here on earth. The Bible tells us in Revelation 21:1 that God is going to make a new heaven and a new earth. There will be nations operating and we will be placed in positions of various capacities. There will be job responsibilities, spheres of oversight, goals to accomplish— things to do (see Revelation 2:26–28; 20:4–6). The kingdom will be the full manifestation of God's government and will operate in perfect righteousness.

Just like good workers get a promotion on the job, so will Christ's faithful stewards get promotions in the kingdom. We just read a Scripture that tells us some will even manage ten cities.

Finally, this faithful steward got a third reward. It was a surprise, a bonus. You'll find it in verse 24. He got the mina that the master had originally given to the third slave. When Jesus Christ comes, He is going to look at those who were not faithful and take away from them what little bit they did have.

You may think that's not fair. But we need to remember one thing. Christ is going to make sure His kingdom resources aren't wasted. For those who fail to grasp an opportunity to participate in kingdom service, Christ will give it to someone else and the unfortunate ones will lose out.

THE LESS PRODUCTIVE
AND THE WORTHLESS STEWARD

The second servant also had a good report, although he wasn't as productive as the first. He said, "Your mina, master, has made five minas" (v. 18). So the master told him, "You are to be over five cities" (v. 19).

Did you notice that this servant didn't get any public recognition? He got his five cities, but no "Well done." I believe the reason is that he was only half as faithful as he could have been.

Let me explain. I think this servant possibly represents someone who gets saved at twenty years of age but doesn't get going for the Lord until he's forty. Ultimately, he lives to be sixty. Altogether, he's got twenty "lost" years, in terms of kingdom reward and twenty productive years.

Should this person say at age forty, "I've already lost twenty years; I might as well give up"? No, he should get going at forty and serve Christ effectively until he's sixty. The point is, in any circumstances, always strive to do your best for the kingdom of God. In the end, you will receive the reward you've earned. Make sure you get your five cities, or whatever reward is coming to you.

Then there's the third servant. He brought his mina and said, "Master, here is your mina, which I kept put away in a handkerchief; for I was afraid of you, because you are an exacting man" (vv. 20–21).

All this man gave was a poor excuse. In so many words, he said, "Master, I just want you to know I didn't lose your money. I kept it safe and sound under my mattress. I took the resources you gave me and stored them away, because you are a hard master."

During the time the master was away, this guy had been playing both ends against the middle. Here was his reasoning: "I am not going to break my neck serving my master. He is going away on some long trip. He may not even come back. He may forget all about me. In the meantime, I've got my own business to tend to. I've got my own house to build and money to make and talents to use. But just in case he does come back, I'll make sure I don't lose what he gave me. I'll play it safe and hide his mina. And if he doesn't come back, I'll keep it for myself since there won't be a record of it in any bank."

What a sad statement. Remember the film *Lilies of the Field* with Sidney Poitier? In this story, his character was building a church for the nuns in a small town. When he asked a local businessman to help, the man said, "I'm not really into religion. I'm not the man." But when they started the building process, this same man came with a hammer and nails and got up on the scaffold to help build the church.

Sidney Poitier asked him why he was doing this, since he wasn't a religious man. The man said, "Just in case what these nuns believe is right, I want to have something to show."

In the parable, that's what the third servant was saying. "I'm not going to get fanatical about this service stuff. But just in case my master does return, I want to have

something to show him. I want to have some insurance."
The master told this servant, "By your own words I
will judge you, you worthless slave" (v. 22a). Then he
asked him, "Why did you not put my money in the bank,
and having come, I would have collected it with interest?"
(v. 23).

I'm afraid for the many Christians who can talk about
the grace and goodness of God, who can praise Him for
taking them from nowhere to somewhere, but who are
not giving Him a decent return on His investment in
them. These people are not only failing to return 1,000 or
500 or even 10 percent of their increase to God. Like the
faithless steward, they aren't even producing the 2 or 3
percent they could get down at the local bank. Through
this parable, Jesus is telling us that stewards like that are
no good to Him. In fact, in one translation the worthless
man is called "lazy."

As a result of his lack of dedication, in direct contrast
to the first servant, the lazy steward received a ringing
condemnation. He got no cities. The story revealed that
even the mina he was given was taken away from him. He
received the same amount of credit as profit he produced
for the master—none.

Notice in verse 24 the involvement of the "bystanders" in this man's judgment: "Then [the master] said
to the bystanders, 'Take the mina away from him and give
it to the one who has the ten minas.'" I don't know how
God is going to do it, but somehow the results of Christ's
judgment seat will be visible to everyone.

Woe to anyone who is simply wearing the name of Christ as a decoration instead of bringing honor to His name. Everyone will know. If we have nothing to bring to Christ that can withstand the fire, other believers at His judgment seat will be aware of it.

That's why I think there are going to be some big surprises on that day. People might say such things as, "But I thought so-and-so was a good Christian. He always came to church with his Bible under his arm. He was al ways saying 'Praise the Lord.'" While that may have been so, in reality, if there was no depth to an individual's commitment, it will become quite obvious on that day.

Look at how Jesus summarized this parable about stewardship: "I tell you that to everyone who has, more shall be given, but from the one who does not have, even what he does have shall be taken away" (Luke 19:26). We saw this in the abundant reward of the first servant and the judgment of the third servant. Friend, the same holds true not only in all of life but particularly with your finances. The most important thing that you can do on the path to financial victory is to operate according to the biblical principles of stewardship.

Since this is the case, where do you start in making your financial stewardship productive and pleasing to God?

Well, a good place to start is by turning the words of Hebrews 12:28 into your constant prayer: "Therefore, since we receive a kingdom which cannot be shaken, let us show gratitude, by which we may offer to God an acceptable service with reverence and awe."

Go to God daily and pray, "Lord, thank You for the certainty of Your kingdom. Help me to show my gratitude to You by serving You faithfully today and every day. My desire is to honor You with how I use the money You have given to me. Give me the grace I need to make the most of what You have loaned to me. Help me to use my finances to prioritize Your agenda over mine."

> IT IS CLEAR FROM SCRIPTURE THAT IF PEOPLE WISH TO PROSPER THEY MUST BE WILLING TO WORK HARD.

With faith that God hears your prayer, don't negate your petition by being like the worthless steward who was called lazy. Work in such a way so as to do everything that you can to set yourself up for an increase. God will answer your heartfelt prayer and will oftentimes use your personal productivity to create wealth for you. Laziness is not the path to bearing financial fruit. The book of Proverbs tells us,

> Poor is he who works with a negligent hand, but the hand of the diligent makes rich. (10:4)

The soul of the sluggard craves and gets nothing, but the soul of the diligent is made fat. (13:4)

In all labor there is profit, but mere talk leads only to poverty. (14:23)

The sluggard does not plow after the autumn, so he begs during the harvest and has nothing. (20:4)

Those are just a few of the verses concerning what God has to say regarding laziness. It is clear from Scripture that if people wish to prosper they must be willing to work hard. And if they are unwilling to work, they should not eat (see 2 Thessalonians 3:10). Lazy people are present- rather than future-oriented. Anyone who wants to please God and reap His rewards must begin by taking responsibility for themselves and their families.

When the lazy poor can receive handouts that require little or no productivity on their part, then we aid and abet their economic deterioration, as well as our own. It seems as though, today, everyone wants to get rich but few are willing to do their due diligence and pursue wealth honorably.

Yet God has clearly revealed that one of the major contributing factors to living a life of financial fruitfulness is personal productivity. God is looking for those who have a righteous work ethic and a desire to please Him with their finances. If that is you, know that you can trust Him. He will reveal to you things to do or methods to

use that will produce wealth when you are living according to His covenant.

> ## IT'S NOT WHAT YOU KNOW.
> ## IT'S **WHO** YOU KNOW.

For a biblical example, consider this occasion. Peter had
fished all night long and caught nothing. Fishing was his
profession; his trade. However, when Jesus came, He told
Peter to put his net on the other side of the boat. Since Peter
was willing to trust Jesus' word and follow His instructions,
albeit grudgingly, he reaped the reward of a major catch.

The Lord has a way of taking your work and increas-
ing its results when you make Him and His precepts first
in your life. He will bless you when He knows that the
blessing will be used for more than you; that you will extend it to advance His kingdom.

Do you want to know the secret of how to get ahead
in life? It's not what you know. It's *Who* you know. If you
know God and have a deep, abiding relationship with
Him that honors Him tangibly with your resources, He
can give you ideas on how to produce wealth that no one
would have ever considered. After all, God made everything and He knows the surest way to bless you.

A note of caution, though, as you look to the Lord

and His blessings. While you are waiting, one thing to avoid is the spirit of envy. This is a sinful attitude that hinders kingdom economic growth. Envy goes a step further than jealousy. Jealousy says, "I am upset because you have something that I don't have." Envy says, "Not only am I upset about what you have, but since I don't have it, I will either make sure you don't have it or at least you will not enjoy it."

Don't get caught in this trap. Envy sets in motion a whole string of events that try to deny people the legitimate ownership of what they have. Subsequently, it creates all manner of accompanying sin. Clearly defining envy as an illegitimate passion in the Bible, Paul said that the wicked are marked by envy (see Romans 1:29), among other immoral behaviors. In Romans 13:13, he further added that envy must not characterize the people of God.

The spirit of envy is actually a theological problem because it stems from a false view of God. When we are envious, we are saying that God is either not sovereign or not good. In our view, God has failed to give us what we think we ought to have. Subsequently, we become envious if someone else has it. This dire condition identifies the root of envy as a faulty, weak, and entirely false view of God.

If you want to seek Him and His blessings in your financial life, a proper starting point is an accurate view of God's sovereignty—along with contentment with what He has chosen to provide.

HONOR GOD WITH
YOUR FINANCES AND EXPECT A RETURN

When a farmer plants his rows of crops, he expects them to grow. He looks forward to receiving a reward for his labor. Similarly, God wants you to expect to be blessed. If you will function according to the financial principles that He gives you, He wants you to expect to receive a reward both now and in eternity.

There is nothing wrong with expecting God to keep His Word to you when you do what He says. It's what I like to call holding God hostage to His Word. Proverbs tells us, "The generous man will be prosperous, and he who waters will himself be watered" (11:25). In other words, what goes around comes around. If and when you honor God with your finances, He sets you up to be blessed financially.

Moreover, the surest way to achieve financial victory is to follow every "jot and tittle" of God's Word on the proper use of money, beginning with generosity. In the book of Luke, we read about this same principle. "Give, and it will be given to you. They will pour into your lap a good measure—pressed down, shaken together, and running over. For by your standard of measure it will be measured to you in return" (Luke 6:38).

The truth you can bank on from God's Word is this: *Giving is the pathway to receiving.* To put it another way, if you want something from God, you must first give something to God. He wants to honor you, but only if He is honored by you.

Most Christians have it backwards. They say, "Lord, give to me and then I will give to You." Yet God is saying, "Give to Me and then I will give to you." The fundamental difference between you and God is that He is trustworthy—you are not. Sadly, too many times God will give to His children and then they will walk away from Him.

The truth is, whether we do or not, God will always keep His word. It is impossible for Him to lie, and He has already said that this is what He will do. That's why we are told to, "Honor the Lord from your wealth and from the first of all your produce; so your barns will be filled with plenty and your vats will overflow with new wine" (Proverbs 3:9–10).

Scripture also tells us that God owns the cattle on a thousand hills (see Psalm 50:10). From the Word of God, we also hear, "'The silver is Mine and the gold is Mine,' declares the Lord of hosts" (Haggai 2:8). What a great and powerful God we serve!

In fact, God owns everything, even that which belongs to the unrighteous. From Scripture, we read, "The wealth of the sinner is stored up for the righteous" (Proverbs 13:22b). When God observes you following His principles with regard to the stewardship of money, He gives you more than enough in return. He even has a way of giving you what other people have worked for, toiled for, and invested, if you will but obey His precepts concerning your money. He can set you on the path to financial victory if you will simply follow His Word. What a great concept, and what a great God!

This is the principle of honoring God first and then allowing Him to measure out in return what measure you will receive. Ephesians 6:8 tells us, "knowing that whatever good thing each one does, this he will receive back from the Lord." When you understand this principle and do good with your money, you honor God in the way you both use it and give it. Scripture guarantees that you will "receive back from the Lord."

> # WE MUST REALIZE THAT
> # A BLESSING GOES FAR BEYOND
> # RECEIVING MONETARY GAIN.

On the other hand, the reverse is true as well. When you give God your leftovers, whatever money remains after you've satisfied yourself and invested in everything that you want, you will receive back His leftovers as well.

THE REWARD OF ENJOYMENT

A blessing in the Bible is the enjoyment of God's divine favor. His blessing is not just about having stuff, or accumulating more money. I know numerous people who have gotten more money only to have also gotten more misery.

We must realize that a blessing goes far beyond receiving monetary gain. It includes the ability and freedom to enjoy your financial gain. Scripture tells us, "It is the blessing of the Lord that makes rich, and *He adds no sorrow to it*" (Proverbs 10:22, emphasis mine). This verse is critical when exploring the area of financial victory because to achieve victory in your finances involves much more than simply seeing an increase in your bank account. It gives you the ability to extend that increase for the sake of God's kingdom.

If you experience a financial increase in your life and yet you do not possess the ability to enjoy it, you have not been blessed. In fact, Scripture tells us that money, or the love and pursuit of it, can lead you away from God and His blessings in your life. We read, "For the love of money is a root of all sorts of evil, and some by longing for it have wandered away from the faith and pierced themselves with many griefs" (1 Timothy 6:10).

Both Christians and the unsaved alike can have a lot of money and still be miserable. Why? Because money, in and of itself, is not the blessing. The ability to enjoy and extend financial favor to others is the blessing.

Paul understood the meaning of being blessed. That's why he was able to say of himself, "I have learned to be content in whatever circumstances I am. I know how to get along with humble means, and I also know how to live in prosperity" (Philippians 4:11–12a). Whether things were plenty or scarce, Paul knew contentment because he knew that Christ was with him, giving him the power to endure in all circumstances.

For instance, a person can be happy in an apartment with God and miserable in a five-bedroom house without Him. The blessing has to do with more than simply having money and material things. It has to do with the ability to fully reap the benefits of peace and contentment with what you have been given.

THE REWARD OF INTIMACY

There is another reward that comes from biblical stewardship. You can expect that when you are in a crisis —and you pray to God for help—He will rescue you.

In the book of Psalms, the psalmist calls for the people of God to: "Offer to God a sacrifice of thanksgiving and pay your vows to the Most High" (50:14). He is admonishing believers to give to God with a heart of gratitude. When we give out of that which He has given to us, God gives us this assurance, "Call upon Me in the day of trouble; I shall rescue you, and you will honor Me" (Psalm 50:15).

Many Christians today are calling on God and not getting an answer because He is not being honored with their finances. When prayer is mixed with following the biblical principles of stewardship, God answers. If you feel like you are praying all of the time but your prayers are reaching the ceiling and stopping there, consider what you are giving to God. Think about how you manage your money. Does it reflect the utmost respect for God? Are you giving Him out of the first of what you receive? Do you make your financial decisions based on His principles, advancing His kingdom, and showing Him honor?

Financial victory is much more comprehensive than simply having extra money in the bank or a retirement account. Living a life of biblical financial victory extends itself into all areas of your life. It even reaches into your prayer life. When you give to God, He will hear and respond to your prayers when you need Him the most.

In the book of Acts, we read about a centurion named Cornelius. God responded to this man not only because of his prayers but because his prayers were mixed with giving. We are introduced to Cornelius at the beginning of chapter ten, where we read,

> Now there was a man at Caesarea named Cornelius, a centurion of what was called the Italian cohort, a devout man and one who feared God with all his household, *and gave many alms* to the Jewish people and prayed to God continually (Acts 10:1–2, emphasis mine).

We learn many things about Cornelius in this brief introduction; mainly, that he was a devout man who gave much. Because of his giving, God sent an answer to his prayers. Later on in the chapter we read,

Cornelius said, "Four days ago to this hour, I was praying in my house during the ninth hour; and behold, a
man stood before me in shining garments, and he
said, 'Cornelius, your prayer has been heard and *your*
alms have been remembered before God'" (Acts 10:30–31,
emphasis mine).

Giving is a powerful thermometer that measures the
temperature of the intimacy in your relationship with
God. What you do with your money is one of the quick-
est revealers of what you value and what you hold close
in life. When you demonstrate that you value and honor
God and the advancement of His kingdom, He pays attention to your needs at the highest level.

There is a familiar verse that is often quoted in relationship to God taking care of us as believers. It was
penned out of the context of financial giving. In his letter to the church at Philippi, Paul wrote, "My God will
supply all your needs according to His riches in glory in
Christ Jesus" (Philippians 4:19).

Christians often quote this verse as a blanket statement for blessings, yet they do so without placing it in
the context in which it was originally made. Actually, this
truth was written in response to the principle of giving.
Without living according to the principle that precedes it,
the promise cannot be claimed. It is interlinked with the
context in which it was stated.

So connected is the principle of provision linked to
giving in the Bible that Paul clearly told the church at

Philippi the reason he sought financial assistance from them was not solely for him to do what God had called him to do, but it was so that they would be blessed. He wrote, "Not that I seek the gift itself, but I seek for the profit which increases to your account" (Philippians 4:17).

Paul told those who were giving to support the advancement of God's kingdom that he wanted them to give because it would ultimately help them even more than it helped him. They would be blessed, not only financially but also emotionally, spiritually, and relationally. In other words, he was saying to believers that they would reap what they sowed. In fact, they would ultimately reap more.

The promise still stands today. It isn't that God will supply our financial needs according to His riches in glory. The promise is that God will supply *all* our needs according to His riches in glory. Now, it doesn't mean that God meets any taste for greed, but it does mean that He will meet the needs of those who invest into His kingdom.

THE LAW OF SOWING AND REAPING

God makes a direct tie to how you treat others with how He treats you. He makes a clear connection between the usefulness you generate with what you have and the increase that He gives to you. In Christian circles, this is typically known as the law of sowing and reaping. We read in Proverbs,

There is one who scatters, and yet increases all the
more, and there is one who withholds what is justly
due, and yet it results only in want. The generous man
will be prosperous, and he who waters will himself be
watered. He who withholds grain, the people will curse
him, but blessing will be on the head of him who sells
it. He who diligently seeks good seeks favor, but he
who seeks evil, evil will come to him (11:24–27).

Birds fly because flying is intrinsic to birds. Water is
wet because wetness is intrinsic to water. Fire is hot because heat is intrinsic to fire. Sowing reaps because reaping is intrinsic to sowing. Whatever it is that you sow, you
also reap in return. As we just read, "he who waters will
himself be watered." According to the biblical principles
of stewardship—when you give—you also get.

There are six principles related directly to the law of
sowing and reaping that I want to cover as we wrap up
this section on the rewards of stewardship. If you will
apply these principles to your finances, you will reap financial victory in your life.

PRINCIPLE #1: YOUR HARVEST DEPENDS ON WHETHER YOU SOW

The first principle is that your harvest depends on
whether you sow. If there is no sowing of seeds, you cannot
expect a harvest. There are a lot of Christians who expect a
harvest from God in their lives related to their finances; yet
they are not sowing any seeds for the kingdom.

These Christians simply do not understand the law of the harvest. Just like in farming, if you want something to come up out of the ground, you have to first put something into the ground. You cannot harvest from seedless ground.

The book of John records Jesus' words, "Truly, truly, I say to you, unless a grain of wheat falls into the earth and dies, it remains alone; but if it dies, it bears much fruit" (John 12:24). For a seed to be sown, you must give up your own wants and desires to nurture that seed. It must "die" to you in order to bear fruit for the kingdom, thus becoming useful to you and others later on.

Sowing is what sets the harvest in motion. Suppose a farmer were to say, "This year I am not going to sow any seeds in my eighty acres of land, but I am trusting God for a full crop of corn because I know that He can do exceedingly abundant over all I can ask or imagine."

If you heard him say that, you would assume that the farmer has lost his mind. He can't expect for his eighty acres of farmland to produce even one stalk of corn if he doesn't take the time and effort to sow seeds first.

Yet this is what many people do with regard to their finances. They come to church, or spend time with God, asking Him to give them a harvest of great financial gain. They do this without being willing to even sow a small seed here or there. But there is no way around it. If you want a harvest, you have to sow seeds accordingly. It's as simple and straightforward as that. Paul

writes about sowing and reaping in his second letter to
the church at Corinth where we read,

> Now this I say, he who sows sparingly will also reap
> sparingly, and he who sows bountifully will also reap
> bountifully. Each one must do just as he has purposed
> in his heart, not grudgingly or under compulsion, for
> God loves a cheerful giver. (2 Corinthians 9:6–7)

> Now He who supplies seed to the sower and bread
> for food will supply and multiply your seed for sow-
> ing and increase the harvest of your righteousness;
> you will be enriched in everything for all liberality. (2
> Corinthians 9:10–11a)

With regard to preparing for the future, here is something else for you to seriously consider. No farmer in his
right mind would eat all of his produce, including all of
his seeds. If he eats all of his produce and all of his seeds,
he has nothing with which to re-seed. Yet that's what a
lot of people do. They get the good things from God that
He supplies. Then they consume it all, leaving nothing
left to sow for the future. Friend, if you eat all of your harvest, there is nothing left to plant for another harvest.

Living a life that bears financial fruit will benefit the
advancement of God's kingdom. There are three key elements of fruit that are helpful in understanding how we
are to manage our money. The first one is that fruit always bears after its own kind. You will never have an

apple tree producing a watermelon. You will never have a papaya tree producing a banana. Fruit resembles and reflects the kind of seed that it comes from.

The second aspect about fruit is that it is always intended to benefit someone else besides itself. You never see a piece of fruit consuming itself, unless it is rotten, which brings us to the third aspect of fruit. Healthy fruit does not consume itself. Rotten fruit is the only kind of fruit that eats itself, making it no good to anyone else.

Bearing financial fruit comes by following biblical principles on money. When you honor God and His kingdom with what you sow, you will reap after His own kind. You will reap according to God's provision, order, and gain. You will reap blessings according to His purposes. You will also position yourself to help others with the increase God has given you. Your financial fruit will continue to bear even more fruit in the lives of those you sow into.

Lastly, you will bear healthy fruit, rather than rotten fruit, when you do not consume all that God has given you solely for yourself. If the latter is the case, it will leave you with nothing to replant.

PRINCIPLE #2: YOUR HARVEST DEPENDS ON WHAT YOU SOW

The second principle toward living a life of financial fruitfulness involves what you sow. We read "Do not be deceived, God is not mocked; for whatever a man sows, this he will also reap" (Galatians 6:7). As a matter of fact, the Bible tells us this historical principle dates all the way back to the beginning of time. From Genesis, we read, "The earth brought forth vegetation, plants yielding seed after their kind, and trees bearing fruit with seed in them, after their kind; and God saw that it was good" (Genesis 1:12).

God set up the world to function in such a way that if you plant a potato seed, you get a potato. Or if you plant a tomato seed, you get tomatoes. Whatever you put in the ground is what comes back up.

Not only does this principle work in the agricultural world, it operates in your life as well. If you sow scarcity in your finances toward God, you will reap scarcity in your finances from God toward you. If you sow generously in your finances toward God, you will reap generously in your finances from God toward you.

In other words, if you plant something bad, don't expect to grow something good. If you plant nothing into God and the advancement of His kingdom and the expansion of His glory on earth, then why are you expecting great things from God? If there is no spiritual investment, why are you expecting a spiritual return?

This explains why so many of our prayers are receiving "nickel" answers because so many of our lives and life choices reflect a "nickel" request. If you give leftovers, you are going to get leftovers. If you give honor, you are going to get honor. You reap what you sow; therefore, you should sow wisely.

Principle #3: Your Harvest Depends on How Much You Sow

The third principle for living out a life of financial fruitfulness involves how much seed you sow. As we saw earlier, "he who sows sparingly will also reap sparingly, and he who sows bountifully will also reap bountifully" (2 Corinthians 9:6). Consequently, you can't put one seed into an eighty-acre plot of land and expect eighty acres worth of crop to grow. It just doesn't work that way. The size of your harvest is determined by the amount you sow. If you want an eighty-acre return then you need to plant eighty acres worth of seed.

The question regarding your finances should never be: What do I want to sow? The question you really need to ask is: What do I want to harvest? Once you determine what you want to harvest, that will determine what you need to sow. If you want big things from God, then honor Him big in your finances. If you only want ordinary things from God, then treat Him like an ordinary God. The bottom line is this: If you sow sparingly, don't expect to reap bountifully.

No farmer sows sparingly who expects to get a bumper crop. Yet it is amazing how many people want a bumper crop from God but will only throw in one seed toward glorifying Him and advancing His kingdom. You wouldn't treat your boss that way if you wanted a bumper paycheck. You wouldn't show up at work one day a week and say, "Hey, at least I showed up once." Not only would you not get your bumper paycheck, but you may even lose your job.

We won't treat men that way; yet so many of us will treat God that way. All the while, we expect Him to bless us. That approach won't work on your job and it definitely won't work with God.

PRINCIPLE #4: YOUR HARVEST DEPENDS ON WHERE YOU SOW

Not only does your financial harvest depend on whether you sow, what you sow, and how much you sow, it also depends on where you sow. If you sow seeds underneath your carpet, you're not going to get a thing to grow there. Your carpet is not a proper environment for growth.

In the parable of the sower, when Jesus speaks of sowing He speaks of sowing in "good soil" (Matthew 13:8). Good soil means investing in the kingdom of God. When you invest in the advancement of the gospel, God's glory and His kingdom, you are sowing in good soil.

Good soil is where people grow in the faith, lives are changed, and the poor are enhanced or enabled to work for what they need. In turn, when you invest your seed in good soil, God takes notice and will multiply it according to your investment. He will continue to bless you and enable you to do even more.

PRINCIPLE #5: YOUR HARVEST DEPENDS ON WHEN YOU SOW

One of the reasons why so many Christians struggle with understanding the principles of giving with regard to sowing and reaping is because we have become so industrialized in our thinking. Most of us don't have a clue about what it means to plant a crop and wait for it to harvest. We don't know what it's like to live in an agrarian community. This makes it difficult to grasp the principle of when to sow financial seeds and then wait patiently for a return on our investment.

> WE WANT INSTANTANEOUS
> EVERYTHING THESE DAYS AND,
> THEREFORE, WE FAIL TO WAIT
> PATIENTLY ON THE HARVEST
> FOR WHAT WE HAVE SOWN.

In an effort to become effective stewards with what we have, it would benefit us to become "country-oriented" Christians in our mindset. Now, I admit that I'm a city boy from Baltimore, so farming concepts are foreign to me. But it is essential that we make the effort to understand, embrace, and apply them in our lives because they play an important role in our financial victory.

As industrialized Christians who live in a world where everything is expected to happen in an instant, we have lost sight of a very important virtue. It is the virtue of patience. We want instantaneous everything these days and, therefore, we fail to wait patiently on the harvest for what we have sown. Many Christians will sow by honoring God with their finances, but when they don't see an immediate return on their investment, they give up and assume that sowing must not work.

On the other hand, no farmer plants in the spring and expects a harvest in the spring. It just doesn't work that way. When my son Anthony was much younger, he was given a project at school where he was instructed to plant a seed, water it, and take care of it. Anthony faithfully planted his seed and tended to it the first day and night. But the very next day, Anthony came into my room crying. I asked him what was wrong, and he asked me to come and look at his seed. When I looked at his cup of dirt, I asked him again what was wrong.

He said, "My seed. It didn't do anything. There's nothing there."

Anthony didn't yet understand a very important lesson. When you plant a seed, there is always a period where you have to wait before you experience the fruit, or growth, from that seed. You never get your harvest the day after you sow. Waiting on a harvest requires patience during the time in which growth occurs.

The same holds true in our finances and honoring God. That is why Paul writes to us not to give up when we don't see immediate results. "Let us not lose heart in doing good, for in due time *we will reap* if we do not grow weary" (Galatians 6:9, emphasis mine).

Some Christians have stopped planting financial

seeds simply because they have not seen a harvest come fast enough. But the harvest will not happen until "due time." Due time simply means the right time for that particular seed. All seeds do not demand the same time to grow, but they all demand the right time to bear fruit.

God knows just where you are in your growth cycle and will allow your seed to produce its harvest at just the right time. Leave the timing in His hands, and don't give up simply because you do not see immediate results. Hang in there, your harvest is coming. Patient sowing takes faith, and faith pleases God.

Principle #6: Your Harvest Depends on Why You Sow

The difference between the prosperity gospel and legitimate, biblical prosperity is motivation. Prosperity theology teaches a philosophy of gain in the name of God that is regularly detached from spiritual development. As a result, it promotes the idea that material gain can take precedence over spiritual growth.

God isn't opposed to material gain, but He is opposed to allowing material gain that seeks to leave Him out. God is all about God. His purposes encompass His own glory and recognition, along with the advancement of His kingdom. When you make God's goals your goals, He has every reason to respond to your requests.

Recently, I was with a pastor who had a small church. And yet, despite their own financial limitations, they decided as a church to practice the theology of sowing.

Whenever they were in a position to help a new church that was struggling to get on its feet, this pastor's church would take up an offering for that particular church. Several times, they would send over $10,000 from his church's offering to the other church. The pastor told me that they were "planting seeds."

Not long after the pastor's church decided to help out other churches in need, the congregation received an anonymous gift of $500,000. All they did was follow the biblical principle of sowing in order to bring God glory. Then God opened the heavens and poured down a half million dollars on them. The bottom line is, God gets behind that which brings Him the greatest glory and advances His kingdom.

Let me illustrate my point in another way. One day a man was in the desert and was very thirsty. It had been a long time since he'd found anything to drink. Up ahead of him, he saw a small hut next to a well. The man knew that he would die soon if he did not get some water.

A small jar rested next to the well with a note beside it. The note read,

> Stranger, the water in the jar is not to drink. It is to prime the pump of the well. When you prime the pump, you will get more water than you can ever drink. When you are done drinking, leave the jar full of water for the next person.

The man was in a catch-22. He could drink the water in the jar and survive for a few more days. Or he could risk losing the water altogether if he tried to prime the pump and it didn't work. But if the pump worked, he would have more than enough water to survive as long as he needed it.

After thinking it over, the man decided to pour the water into the pump. This would expand the leather of the pump, allowing it to grip and begin producing water. When he began to pour the water in, though, nothing happened. He poured more water and still nothing happened. The man began to break out into a cold sweat because he was pouring down a hole the very thing that could save him.

Then just before he was about to run out of water altogether, he saw water begin to gush out of the pump. The man was able to fill up anything and everything he could find that would hold water because the pump never ran dry.

Friend, God has more resources and money than you could ever need. He has a well that is bigger than your wildest dreams. Yet, He is asking you one thing: Are you going to prime the pump with what He's given you? Or are you going to keep it for yourself? You are allowed to keep it for yourself if you want. It's just that—when it's gone—it's gone. But if you prime the pump by giving back to God what is already His, He will supply more than enough for you.

PICK UP THE PACE

I used to play the game of Monopoly all the time. I still love to play it because, when I do, I get to own land. Playing Monopoly gives me the opportunity to pretend as though I am a real estate mogul like Donald Trump—buying and selling property.

Beware, though, if you're playing with me, you'd better not let me get Boardwalk and Park Place. If I get those two properties, I show no mercy. Once I accumulate enough money, I'm going to buy some little green houses for Boardwalk and Park Place.

Then when I buy enough green houses, I'm going to turn those bad boys in for two big red hotels. The property value now escalates, and you'd better hope you can skip over my property and collect another two hundred dollars for passing "Go." Otherwise, I am going to be sitting there waiting on you.

Now let me tell you about the hard part of playing Monopoly. It's when the game is over. Then I have to give up all my make-believe property and money, close the box, and go back to the real world.

Friend, someday, they are going to close the box on you and me. We are going to leave this world and go to the real world, the kingdom of God. There we will show what we *really* have. The only thing that will matter on that day is, not what we left behind but, what we have sent on ahead.

The only "property" that will count at Christ's judgment seat is the time, talents, and treasure we invested in things of eternal value. What will matter then is what we did to make a difference for the kingdom.

You may be saying, "Tony, I want to make the most of my stewardship. I want to be an effective servant in the kingdom. But I've lost some time, and I've wasted God's money. What do I do?"

You do the same thing a runner does when he or she falls behind in a race. You have to pick up the pace. You can't worry about the territory you've already covered. Yesterday is gone, but you can pick up the pace today so you can cover more territory tomorrow.

Always remember this. The kingdom of God has only one Ruler. But it has room for an unlimited number of servants. What Jesus Christ is looking for are faithful stewards who will say to Him, "Lord, You are first in my time, my talents, and my treasure. Help me to make Your kingdom agenda my agenda. Help me to make an eternal difference for You."

When you're ready to pray that prayer and live it, you're in line to hear Jesus say, "Well done" on that day.

VICTORY

We live in a nation known for the freedom that it offers. We have freedom of religion, freedom of speech, freedom of assembly, freedom of the press, and others.

However, the one freedom that very few Americans are experiencing today is the freedom from debt. Americans are drowning in a sea of debt. Many have become slaves to the lenders in today's economy. As we read in Proverbs, "The rich rules over the poor, and the borrower becomes the lender's slave" (Proverbs 22:7). For these people, the familiar credit card name, Visa, can be translated as "Volunteering for Institutional Slavery Always."

Too many consumers are like the Seven Dwarfs who lived with Snow White. We leave for work every morning

singing a similar song, "I owe, I owe, so off to work I go."
Someone once said, "Money talks, and it regularly says
'Good-bye!'"

Here is a startling fact that I discovered on CNN
Money, a financial website: In 2012, the average American household with at least one credit card now has close
to $15,950 in credit card debt alone.[1] That's not counting
automobile loans, student loans, and home mortgages.
Sadly, for most wage earners, debt has become a way of
life. There are now three groups of people in our nation:
The Haves, the Have-Nots, and the Have-Not-Paid-For-
What-They-Have. Instead of living for the future, people are now paying for the past. Debt has become the new
addiction.

Whatever debt rules, debt ruins. Marriages have ended
in divorce over fighting about bills and money. Dreams
have been sidelined because some people must focus their
time and attention on trying to stay afloat in a sea of debt.
Homes have been lost, businesses have gone bankrupt,
and families have been destroyed over this nemesis called
debt.

While there is a lot of bad news about debt, there is
some good news as well. That is, you don't have to be a
slave to debt. There is a way out. God has given you a
way to completely pay off all of the debt that you have,
if you will simply follow His principles.

The Bible tells us that it is abnormal for a Christian to
live in debt, where your liabilities exceed your assets. God
says that if you follow Him and obey His commands, you

will be the lender and not the borrower. Living under His covenant makes us the head and not the tail, in the way God ordained it to be. We read,

> The Lord will open for you His good storehouse, the heavens, to give rain to your land in its season and to bless all the work of your hand; and you shall lend to many nations, but you shall not borrow. The Lord will make you the head and not the tail, and you only will be above, and you will not be underneath, if you listen to the commandments of the Lord your God, which I charge you today, to observe them carefully. (Deuteronomy 28:12–13)

The Word of God is precise. Therefore, if debt is a way of life for you, it means you and God are not on the same page. Debt is more than a financial issue. It is a spiritual issue. In fact, David pointed out that those who do not repay their debt are wicked. He wrote, "The wicked borrows and does not pay back" (Psalm 37:21a).

God's Word teaches us this important truth about managing our finances. If believers don't know how to wisely handle the money that God has given them, unwise use of their funds will actually cut them off from future blessing. We read about it,

> He who is faithful in a very little thing is faithful also in much; and he who is unrighteous in a very little thing is unrighteous also in much. Therefore if you

have not been faithful in the use of unrighteous
wealth, who will entrust the true riches to you? (Luke
16:10–11)

A refusal to handle God's money God's way can cut
off any request you have of Him for greater things. As we
have seen throughout this book, financial victory is not
just about money. It is a spiritual worldview of stewardship that includes money.

This spiritual worldview involves three words that will
assist you in getting out of debt, successfully managing
your money, and living a life of financial victory. If you
will begin to fully apply these three simple words, in this
order, you will begin to see your financial life change—
based on God's Word.

The three words that can have a profound impact on
your life, if you will abide by them are: *Give, Save, Spend.*
Your path to financial victory is completely tied to what
those three words mean for the kingdom of God.

STEP 1: GIVE

The first word is one that I have touched on quite a
bit already in the earlier chapters. It is the concept of giving. Unless and until you get this part of your financial
stewardship right, you will not experience the fullness of
the financial blessings that God has in store for you. This
principle is the foundation upon which all else is built.

Unfortunately in Christian circles today, we are experiencing a condition that I call "Cirrhosis of the Giver." While American Christians control over 70% of the world's Christian wealth, the average American only gives 2.6% of his or her income.[2] Furthermore, only 5–7% of all Christians actually tithe.[3] And we wonder why we are experiencing so much by way of financial struggles, strain, and defeat. When we fail to live out God's principles with regard to stewardship—beginning with giving —we fail to reap God's blessings with regard to reward and provision.

The Hebrew word that we translate as our word "tithe" in the Bible is *ma'as*[4] which simply means "tenth part" or "a payment of a tenth." In the book of Deuteronomy, God gives us the reason behind the tithe. We read,

> You shall surely tithe all the produce from what you sow, which comes out of the field every year. You shall eat in the presence of the Lord your God, at the place where He chooses to establish His name, the tithe of your grain, your new wine, your oil, and the firstborn of your herd and your flock, *so that you may learn to fear the Lord your God always.* (Deuteronomy 14:22–23, emphasis mine)

The tithe reflected and demonstrated a fear of God. Scripture is replete with the importance of fearing God. Proverbs tells us, "The fear of the Lord is the beginning of wisdom" (Proverbs 9:10a). The wisest man who ever lived, Solomon, sums up the fear of God as the most important thing that we can do when he writes, "The con-clusion, when all has been heard, is: fear God and keep His commandments, because this applies to every person" (Ecclesiastes 12:13).

Therefore, giving a tenth of what you have to God acts as a teacher who instructs you on how to do the most important thing that you can do: fear God. Scripture says that the tithe was given *"so that you may learn to fear the Lord your God always."* When we fear God, we show Him the reverence and respect for all that He is to us. Having a fear of God means that our hearts are turned toward pleasing Him and ensures our motives are pure when we give.

IN THE BOOK OF MATTHEW, JESUS AFFIRMED THE GIVING OF THE TITHE.

Yet some people argue that the tithe was given under the Law, and we are no longer under the Law. Usually these are the same people who don't want to give a tithe to God and choose to keep their money for themselves. What they fail to recognize is that the tithe was given be-fore the Law was instituted.

From the creation of time, God has always held some-thing back that was His in order to give humanity an opportunity to demonstrate that they fear Him and respect His sovereignty. In the garden of Eden, God instructed Adam and Eve that they could eat from every tree except for the Tree of the Knowledge of Good and Evil. Through this restriction, Adam and Eve were being taught "to fear the Lord God always" by recognizing His ownership and authority.

Moreover, specifically related to the tithe, we read in Genesis 14 that before Moses ever gave the Law, Abraham gave a tithe. We read,

> Melchizedek king of Salem brought out bread and wine; now he was a priest of God Most High. He blessed him and said, "Blessed be Abram of God Most High, Possessor of heaven and earth; and blessed be God Most High, who has delivered your enemies into your hand." *He gave him a tenth of all.* (Genesis 14:18–20, emphasis mine)

Abraham (then Abram) gave a tenth, *a tithe,* to the priest of God Most High, Melchizedek. From this Scripture, clearly we find evidence that the tithe preceded the Mosaic law.

Going further, chapter 7 of Hebrews reveals that the priesthood of Melchizedek continues on to Jesus Christ because our Lord is "according to the order of Melchizedek" (Hebrews 7:17). In the same way that Melchizedek covered and blessed Abraham, receiving a tenth from him (see Hebrews 7:1–8), Jesus, our great

High Priest, through a better covenant, covers us and rightly owns a tenth of all that we have (see Hebrews 7:20–22).

In the book of Matthew, Jesus affirmed the giving of the tithe. In fact, in His statements of condemnation to the Jewish leaders with regard to their hypocritical hearts (Matthew 23:23), He chided them for not giving even more than the tithe. Never did Jesus negate the tithe—He added to it.

Unmistakably, the spiritual principle of the tithe didn't stop with the Law because it didn't start with the Law. It started with Abraham and continued into the Priesthood of Jesus Christ. As followers of Christ, we are Abraham's descendants. Paul explained our heritage, "If you belong to Christ, then you are Abraham's descendants, heirs according to promise" (Galatians 3:29). Being his descendants, we are also to follow in the spiritual principle of the tithe, not to Melchizedek as to whom Abraham gave, but to Jesus Christ—who is the fulfillment of the Melchizedeken Priesthood.

Through all of this evidence, it is important for us to understand that the giving of tithes transcends the Law. The spiritual principle, *"so that you may learn to fear the Lord your God always,"* carries into the church age, as we are admonished to "fear God" (1 Peter 2:17).

The reason why so many believers are uncovered today is because they rob God of what is rightly His. Moreover, as we see in the book of Malachi, to withhold the tithe, and even the offering, is to rob from God what is rightly

His. The prophetic question was asked, "Will a man rob God? Yet you are robbing Me! But you say, 'How have we robbed You?' In tithes and offerings" (Malachi 3:8).

> YOU DEMONSTRATE THAT YOU FEAR
> GOD BY SHOWING HIM THAT YOU
> TRUST HIM WITH YOUR POSSESSIONS.

Keep in mind, you can only rob someone if what you are taking is not yours, but belongs to another. Practically speaking, that means many people are robbing God today. Many believers are wearing stolen clothes, driving stolen cars, living in stolen homes, and taking stolen vacations because they have used God's money to buy it. Then after neglecting to honor God with their tithes and offerings, these same people are asking God to bless them. Such behavior can be compared to a thief coming back to the person whom they stole from and asking for more.

What would you say to someone who told you that he or she was going to go downtown and rob the police station? You would tell that person that he or she was out of their mind. Robbing the police station doesn't make sense. Yet countless numbers of believers are doing something just as irrational to God. In a spiritual sense, they are robbing the very One who owns everything and has authority over them and all that they possess. They fail to give God what rightly belongs to Him.

Know this. You don't demonstrate that you love and fear God by shouting "amen" on Sunday morning at your church, raising your hands, or singing praise songs. You demonstrate that you fear God by showing Him that you trust Him with your possessions. As we saw earlier, Proverbs instructs us to, "Honor the Lord from your wealth and from the first of all your produce; so your barns will be filled with plenty" (Proverbs 3:9–10a). God connects the state of your barns (your resources and personal economy) directly to your honor and reverence of Him. Your respect and admiration are tangibly demonstrated to Him through the giving of "your wealth."

When you take God's money and use it for reasons other than what He has determined, God allows your resources to dwindle or be devoured. Do you ever feel like no matter how much money you make, it is never enough? There may be a reason why. From God's Word, we read what the prophet told God's people,

> You are cursed with a curse, for you are robbing Me . . . Bring the whole tithe into the storehouse. . . . Then I will rebuke the devourer for you, so that it will not destroy the fruits of the ground; nor will your vine in the field cast its grapes. (Malachi 3:9–11)

One of the primary reasons that so many believers are in debt today is because their plants are not growing, the locusts have eaten up what they have planted, and their vines are bare. As a Christian, there is a direct correlation between your ability to produce wealth productively and your pattern of giving to God. The Bible tells us that the windows of heaven are closed and the very thing that you are asking heaven to do for you—to grant you increase— is the very thing that heaven is not interested in doing for you just so you can continue to steal from God. Why should God give you more so that you can rip Him off more?

For example, if you gave someone the keys to your car, and he didn't bring back your car, would you then give him the keys to your house? Not likely. If you can't trust that person with your car, you are not going to trust that person with your house. On another note, if you gave $1 to your child and your child lost that $1, would you then go and give him $2? Probably not.

The principle is the same with God. Many Christians want more from God when they are robbing Him of what is already His. God will not give more if the more He gives will not be used to honor Him. However, the reverse of that rule is true as well. Honor God with your wealth, and He will open for you the windows of heaven.

If you don't believe me, believe Him. Test Him. It's easy to join the myriad of others who say, "The tithe is just a part of the Law. We are in the age of grace." These are the very ones who continue to struggle financially.

With this mindset, you are only hurting yourself. God says, "'Test Me now in this,' says the Lord of hosts, 'if I will not open for you the windows of heaven and pour out for you a blessing until it overflows'" (Malachi 3:10). So don't take my word for it, God says to test Him. Give—and you will see what God does in return. He is faithful to His Word.

If you are someone who thinks that you need more money, in actuality, you need to be able to keep the money that you already have. The difficulty occurs if you are putting your money into a pocket full of holes. If this is the case, you will never get ahead.

God addressed this very problem with the Israelites. They were spending their money on bigger and better houses for themselves rather than giving to Him what was due Him. As a result, they were losing what they produced. God told His people,

> Consider your ways! You have sown much, but harvest little; you eat, but there is not enough to be satisfied; you drink, but there is not enough to become drunk; you put on clothing, but no one is warm enough; and he who earns, earns wages to put into a purse with holes. (Haggai 1:5–6)

At the end of the day, the path to financial victory involves honoring God with your finances. If you skip that basic premise, it won't matter what else you do. God has scissors and your pockets will have holes.

I was twenty-two years old when I learned this principle. At the time, all I made was $900 a month. We weren't

just poor—we were "po!" Yet even though all I made was
$900 a month, before we did anything else, $90 of it was
given to God along with an offering on top of it. In giving
the tithe and offering to God, I wasn't just telling Him that
I was willing to give Him my money. I was acknowledg-
ing that God is the Owner and I am the steward—and that
all I have is His.

Friend, what you give to God is not simply about
money, it is about your recognition of God as Owner. You
give first to God because God is first. It's just that simple.
You do as Scripture commands and "first seek the kingdom of God so that all else will be added to you"
(Matthew 6:33, paraphrased).

It is such a basic principle that it amazes me how
many people don't believe it, operate by it, and benefit
from it. God didn't make the road to financial victory a
mystery. He set up a signpost, clearly marked with the
message, "Give to Me. I will protect you, provide for you,
and promote what you do."

Yet so many people say, "Tony, I can't afford to tithe."
To this I reply, "You can't afford not to." You need all the
help you can get, and that help comes from God. Don't
rob God and then expect to experience all that He wishes
to bless you with. You are ripping off the very One who
has the power to help you.

Another question that I often hear with regard to the
tithe is, "Tony, does God want me to tithe off of the gross
or off of the net?" To this I reply, "Do you want God to
bless the gross or the net?" It's your call. God has made it

clear what the solution is. He hasn't hidden the answer. It's up to you whether or not you follow. It's up to you whether or not you position yourself to receive the rewards, or whether you position yourself to live life wearing pockets or carrying purses with holes in them.

The first step to financial victory: Give.

STEP 2: SAVE

We are living in a time of great discontent. People are conducting rapidly dissatisfied lives. A growing sense of displeasure with life is strangling the billfolds of many consumers, as advertisers prey on the weak by offering them yet another new way to achieve proposed happiness.

As a result, enormous debt exists simply because our society is suffering from a lack of contentment. It is one of the main reasons for the national housing fiasco that led to an economic downturn a few years ago. Too many people were trying to buy too many houses that they could not afford. On the other hand, there were too many greedy people selling properties that they ought not to have sold to those people. This combination of mistakes led to a tremendous amount of money being wasted. It also adversely affected all of us economically.

The second step on the path to financial victory involves another unfamiliar word in many circles today: Save. Having savings is the opposite of drowning in debt because saving money is future-oriented while accumulating debt is past-oriented.

Savings involves putting away something for tomorrow while debt involves paying for yesterday. Roughly,
only 33% of Americans have a savings account. Yet biblical principles on money include not only saving for
yourself but also saving for your descendants. We read,
"A good man leaves an inheritance to his children's children" (Proverbs 13:22a). It is not enough to be merely
thinking of yourself with regard to your financial plans;
you are to be making plans for your grandchildren as well.

Yet most Christians today can't even get around to the
grandchildren because they haven't gotten around to their
children. And worse yet, they haven't gotten around to
saving for themselves. Unfortunately, a great number of
believers are one crisis away from bankruptcy.

The greatest biblical illustration of the benefits of saving is found in the book of Genesis. It comes from the life
of Joseph. The principles that Joseph followed while in
Egypt not only blessed him, but they also blessed his family and entire nations.

To summarize this account, Pharaoh suffered under a
disturbing dream that he could not understand. In the first
part of the dream, he saw seven fat cows and seven
scrawny cows. The scrawny cows promptly ate up the fat
cows. In the second part of the dream, he saw seven good
stalks of corn and seven thin stalks of corn. Pharaoh woke
up troubled after seeing the thin corn devour the good
corn.

When Joseph was consulted on the meaning of the
dream, he gave us one of the most profound precepts for

financial victory we could ever follow. Joseph instructed Pharaoh in the following way: He told him there would be seven years of plenty followed by seven years of famine in the land. During the years when there was an abundance of food, Pharaoh should take from the overflow and save it so that when the time came for Egypt and the surrounding nations to suffer want, they would have a surplus to fall back on. Scripture reveals Joseph's instructions,

> Let Pharaoh take action to appoint overseers in charge of the land, and let him exact a fifth of the produce of the land of Egypt in the seven years of abundance. Then let them gather all the food of these good years that are coming, and store up the grain for food in the cities under Pharaoh's authority, and let them guard it. Let the food become as a reserve for the land for the seven years of famine which will occur in the land of Egypt, so that the land will not perish during the famine. (Genesis 41:34–36)

Joseph advised Pharaoh to set aside and save during the years of plenty so that there would be enough to supply everyone's needs in the years of famine. This was great advice and it worked.

Friend, you never know when you are going to run into a month, year, or even a decade of famine. Many people were caught off guard when our nation's economy took a downturn a few years ago. This is because they hadn't learned and followed the principle of living a life of financial victory that includes saving for the future.

Both tithing and saving should be an automatic action where you take from the top of your earnings with no questions asked. Even if you have to start out by only saving a small amount, you still need to do it. You need to begin to develop the habit of saving. Cultivate the virtue of saying no to instant gratification and yes to prolonged stability.

As a matter of fact, everyone should not only be saving for themselves, but they should also teach their children how to save. If a young person were to simply put away $100 in savings every month from the time that they are 18 until the natural time of retirement, and if they were to earn an average of 6% interest for their investment, they would have a lot to use for retirement. They would have saved over $1 million dollars by simply investing $100 a month.

On the other hand, when parents fail to model a healthy and biblical worldview on savings to our children, we see them spend, spend, spend rather than save, save, save. Practically speaking, it is foolish to spend everything that one has and leave nothing for the future.

What would happen if a doctor told you that you were going to die but there was a surgery that could save your life? Then you find out that your insurance doesn't cover the surgery costs of $5,000. Would you find that money somehow? Most likely, you would. You would discover a way to come up with $5,000 because all of a sudden saving this money has become a priority to you. My point is, we make the things happen in our lives that are a priority for us. Without a doubt, your future should be a priority for you.

God gave us an illustration of one of the smallest creatures on earth, whose wisdom concerning saving is much greater than most of ours. He directed us to the ant. We read, "Go to the ant, O sluggard, observe her ways and be wise, which, having no chief, officer or ruler, prepares her food in the summer and gathers her provision in the harvest" (Proverbs 6:6–8).

The ant knows how to gather and store away for later and yet many people today who hold bachelor's, master's, or even higher degrees have not yet learned this principle. And then they wonder why there is so much stress when it comes to the handling of finances.

Many of us are not saving money because we have maxed out our personal budgets. We don't see any surplus to set aside for later because every dollar that comes in is already claimed for something. Our house note, car note, grocery bill, and entertainment bill, along with student loans and other obligations demand full use of what we earn.

However, there are a few practical tips that you can use to cut back on your expenses in an effort to save money. While these do not include all of the money-saving ideas that can put you in a better position for saving, they are what I call my "top ten tips." If you will apply them, they can help you to reduce expenses and manage your money. At the same time, putting these ideas into practice can free you up to save:

1. Pay off your debt starting with the smallest bill first. I know it is easier said than done, but a lot of money these days is going to pay interest on credit cards, thus making it difficult for people to save. Here are some strategies for paying off credit card debt:

   a) The first involves checking with your lender(s) concerning whether they can give you a lower interest rate if you close the account and plan to pay it off.

   b) Another way is to consolidate your credit card debt into one loan that gives you a lower interest rate. Credit card interest rates can run upwards of 20–30 percent, and it is often possible to get a consolidated loan in order to transfer your debt and have more of your monthly payment going to principle and not to interest. Just be careful to either close or do not add more debt to your credit cards once you consolidate your debt elsewhere.

2. Cut back on entertainment bills. Particularly with the invention of cheap or even free ways to view entertainment through Hulu.com, Netflix, and other companies, people do not need to spend so much money each month on a large cable subscription. A lot of what you want to view these days can be accessed through the Internet or through inexpensive rental or subscription plans.

In addition, wisely choose what time you go to the movies. Matinees at a theater often will offer the same viewing experience for less than half the price of an evening show. Just don't blow your savings on overpriced popcorn or soda. Eat before you go so you won't be tempted to buy.

3. Use cash. Rarely these days do you see anyone paying with cash, but using cash as your primary method of payment allows you to know how much you really have available. Once you establish a budget (which we will discuss further in the next section), take out the amount you allocated for food, gas, or anything else that you plan to buy and set aside the cash for those purchases.

Using this method, you will have a more accurate reading on how much you have to spend and will be unable to spend more than you budgeted. When the cash is gone for the month, so is the spending. It will only take one or two months of running out early for you to learn a habit of spending that will help you to not run out in the future.

4. Pay off your car or your home early. You can save a tremendous amount of money simply by making additional payments on any car or home loan that will be applied strictly to the principal on the loan. Once your car or home is paid off, use the extra funds that you save and invest it in your future.

5. If you need to buy a car, choose wisely. At the time of this printing, gas prices are painfully high.

Purchasing a car that conserves gas rather than wastes it is an optimal choice. However, any car that you drive can use less gas simply by how you drive it. Using cruise control while on the highways as well as accelerating slowly rather than quickly can economize the usage of your fuel.

6. Install energy saving lightbulbs throughout your home. It has been shown that replacing high energy bulbs with compact fluorescent lights can trim your electrical bill by nearly 25 percent.

7. Cook at home and eat leftovers. Americans spend roughly a little over a third of their annual food budget on eating out. Not only is eating out frequently a poor choice in the types of processed foods that you have to choose, it is also a poor choice for your wallet. Consider spending more time planning your grocery list, going grocery shopping (when you are not hungry), cooking, and also eating leftovers. Use the extra money that you save on your monthly food bill to go toward savings or paying down your debt.

8. Cancel magazine or newspaper subscriptions. Almost every piece of news information that you need to know can now be found online. Even most magazines can be read online, oftentimes for free.

9. Shop around to make sure that you have the absolutely lowest insurance premium on your home, car, health, or for whatever reason you carry insurance. Insurance companies are fairly

competitive and will often beat another company's price simply to get your business. Do your due diligence in buying insurance and use the money that you save to invest in your savings.

10. Lose weight God's way. Americans spend over $40 billion annually on weight-loss products, equipment, memberships, or surgeries. It is one of the top moneymakers in existence. And yet we wouldn't need to lose weight if we followed the biblical principles of taking care of our bodies as the temple of the Holy Spirit, and not giving in to behaviors of greed, excess, and gluttony.

The basics of losing weight typically involve self-control and discipline. Limit simple carbohydrate and sugar intake while balancing your diet with healthy complex carbohydrates, proteins, and fats, along with consistent exercise. It won't cost much and will produce steady and long-term results.

Walking outside for thirty minutes is free or driving to a nearby park only costs the gas that is used as compared to a membership at a local gym. In addition, many people have bought at-home exercise equipment only to not use it and who are looking to sell it at greatly reduced prices. If you want to invest in an at-home exercise gym, look for used equipment instead of buying new.

FINANCIAL VICTORY COMES THROUGH USING FINANCIAL WISDOM.

There are multiple strategies you can employ in order to cut back on your expenses in an effort to redirect those funds either to pay down your debt or to save. These are just a few. Yet whatever you do, begin the process of saving now. Even if it's just to get you used to the concept until you are able to save a larger portion of your income each month, start now.

At a minimum, you should aim to have three to four months worth of living expenses in a savings account. Money above that should be considered for investment opportunities or retirement funds. God has given you a way to enjoy the material blessings from His hand; yet it is not exclusive of following His principles. Financial victory comes through using financial wisdom. It makes the fear of God the highest priority by honoring Him with how you use the money He gives you.

STEP 3. SPEND

The last area that you should focus on regarding your finances is how you spend. Once you have given to God both the tithe and offerings, and once you have used a

portion of your money for savings, the remainder of what
you have is yours to spend.

But don't go spend it on anything and everything. The
Bible has principles related to your spending habits as
well. The first one I want to touch on briefly is your
budget. You need a budget. Without one, you will not be
able to make the most of your money. More than likely,
you run the risk of spending more than you have.
Proverbs tells us, "The plans of the diligent lead surely to
advantage, but everyone who is hasty comes surely to
poverty" (Proverbs 21:5). God is in the planning business.
He wants to bless your plan.

We also read in Proverbs, "Commit your works to the
Lord and your plans will be established" (Proverbs 16:3).
I am amazed at the number of families I counsel who do
not have a financial plan. Every Christian family should
have a plan for how they expect to spend the resources
that God has given them. If there is no plan, then there
is nothing to ask God to help out with.

If you do not have a financial plan, or a budget, for
where your money will go when it comes in with each
paycheck, you need to make one now. If you already have
one, make sure it lines up with the following principles.
By practicing these precepts, you will live in financial victory. That is not to say you will be a millionaire, but it is
to say that you will have the capacity to enjoy and maximize the financial blessings and resources God has given
you.

Your budget should focus on your needs first. Philippians 4:19

says that God will meet all your needs according to His riches. It doesn't say He will meet all your wants. In 1 Timothy 6:8, Paul wrote that our needs include "food and covering," and with these "we shall be content." He is not saying to avoid having desires, but what Paul is saying is to avoid or stop complaining if your needs are being met. Is there a roof over your head? Are there clothes on your back? Is there food in your stomach? God has promised to meet your needs, and the first portion of your budget should be directed at these things.

Before we move on, let me make a distinction between needs and wants. Many people get confused by the two; yet they are very different. For example, you *need* a car to get to work if you don't have access to public transportation. You may *want* a high-priced luxury vehicle but—that is not a need; that is a want. You need a home to live in that is within your means. You may want a five-bedroom home with three baths on several acres of land. But that is a want and not a necessity.

Be mindful and vigilant not to confuse your wants with your needs. Consider how God is blessing you. Are you currently living in an apartment instead of a home? Then thank God for where you are and that He has provided a place for you to stay. One of the worst things that parents hate to hear is their children complain, especially when their needs are provided for in so many ways.

The same thing happened to God when the Israelites were in the wilderness. Even though He kept their shoes from wearing out, rained down cornflakes from above, and provided water for them out of a rock, they still complained. They wanted meat and the kind of food they had grown accustomed to while in slavery. God was leading them to the Promised Land, full of milk and honey. But since they couldn't see where God was taking them, they constantly whined and complained about where they were.

Examine your thoughts and behavior frequently. Anytime you are complaining more than you are giving thanks—be alert and repent. Also, be careful what you ask for. You may just get it like the Israelites did when they complained about only having manna. When they asked God for meat, He gave them so much meat that they eventually became sick from eating too much of it.

If the essentials of your life are being met, you need to thank and praise God because there are a lot of people who don't even have that. Countless people don't have access to clean, running water, transportation, or even food at many times. They wish they were in your shoes. There is nothing that irritates God more than people who are not grateful for what He has given. Start your budget by planning for your needs, but determine what those needs are by using common sense, wisdom, and self-control.

After your needs are met, move on to include your wants in your budget. Your wants go beyond your needs and reflect a level known as desire. You need clothes, but you may want custom made or designer brands. You need food; however, you may want filet mignon and baked potatoes instead of pork and beans. If, after tithing, giving, saving, and meeting your needs, you are then able to satisfy some of your wants in your budget, then plan for how to have those things without going into debt to get them.

Before you decide to make your next purchase, though, I would like to ask you to do something. In fact, if you have a family, take your whole family along. Go to the nearest junkyard and take a tour.

> ABOVE ALL ELSE, MAKE SURE
> THAT YOUR NEEDS COME BEFORE
> YOUR WANTS, OR YOU MAY
> END UP LOSING YOUR NEEDS AT
> THE EXPENSE OF YOUR WANTS.

Do you know what you will see? You will see the remnants of stuff that matters to most people. You will see cars that people used to brag about or spend their Saturday afternoons waxing. You will see dolls that have no arms that once were a highly desirable plaything on Christmas morning. You will see tools that people used to monkey around with now turned into scrap. You will find stuff that people poured their lives into that has no eternal value at all.

My point is that a visit to a junkyard can give you a

sharper perspective and could help you to make wiser purchasing decisions in your life.

Above all else, make sure that your needs come before your wants, or you may end up losing your needs at the expense of your wants. And don't forget to leave room in your budget for helping others. The greatest command is to love God with all of your heart (Matthew 22:37). The second greatest command involves the love of others (Matthew 22:39). If God has blessed you with financial gain in any way, it is so that He can use it to be a blessing to others as well.

Remember, the definition of a blessing is being able to enjoy and extend the favor of God in your life. If it stops with you, it's not a blessing. God blesses in order for you to bless. Plan to bless. Leave room in your budget for ways to help others. You will be amazed at how great it feels to be able to assist someone in need. We read,

> In everything I showed you that by working hard in this manner you must help the weak and remember the words of the Lord Jesus, that He Himself said, "It is more blessed to give than to receive." (Acts 20:35)

If you invest in others with the resources God has given you, blessings will come your way. It is a guarantee. Give, save, and learn how to be content with what you have. Use your money wisely, plan a budget for the income you receive, and you will be walking on the path to financial victory.

However, if you are facing a situation of mounting debt, apply the method I mentioned previously. Remember to take your smallest bill and pay it off first. I recommend that you also cut up your credit cards so you won't be tempted to use them again until you are in a position of living steadily and wisely with your finances. When you pay off your smallest bill, take the money you were using to pay on it and combine it with the payment on your next smallest bill to pay it off. Continue that cycle until you have paid off all of your debt.

Another possibility is to sell some of your possessions to help pay off your debt. There is nothing wrong with having things unless you can't pay your bills and the money that God has given you is going to interest on accumulated debt. That is when it's time to see what you can sell in order to pay what you owe.

As you faithfully and diligently apply yourself, God will be with you every step of the way. The writer of Hebrews reminds us, "Make sure that your character is free from the love of money, being content with what you have; for He Himself has said, 'I will never desert you, nor will I ever forsake you'" (Hebrews 13:5).

BIBLICAL EXAMPLE OF
GETTING OUT OF DEBT

In the book of 2 Kings, we read about a biblical example of a woman in debt. Her husband had died and the authorities were getting ready to take her children to

debtor's prison for what she owed. She had no solution
to her problem. As a single parent, she had to deal with
creditors constantly knocking at her door. The creditors
didn't care that she was alone and had no way to get them
their money. All they knew was that she wasn't paying
her bills.

Desperate, the woman sought spiritual help. She went
to the prophet. God honored this woman's heart in seek-
ing out a spiritual solution to her financial problem. The
prophet instructed her to go to her neighbors and ask
them to give her all of the empty pots that they had in
their houses. He told her to take anything her neighbors
had to spare, close her door, and then pour her oil in
them.

The problem was that this lady had only a small
amount of oil to pour. She could have easily said to the
prophet that his solution didn't make sense. But in faith,
she trusted God instead and did what she was told. After
gathering the empty pots, the single woman went into
her home and began to pour from the only jar of oil she
had.

As she began to pour, she saw that the oil would not
run out. All she had was a little, but God took her little
when she responded in faith and created much. We read
that the woman said to her son, "'Bring me another vessel.'
And he said to her, 'There is not one vessel more.' And
the oil stopped. Then she came and told the man of God.
And he said, 'Go, sell the oil and pay your debt, and you
and your sons can live on the rest'" (2 Kings 4:6–7).

The prophet had given the woman the secret to her financial success. She would not have known it had she not sought him out and followed his instructions. No one could have come up with such a seemingly impossible way for her to pay off her debt, except for the prophet of God who knew it would work.

Friend, God has a plan for you. If you are struggling with debt today, take the time and the effort to seek Him. He has a plan to bring you to financial victory. I can't tell you the exact details of that plan because His ways are higher than our ways and His thoughts are higher than our thoughts.

But what I can tell you is that, if you will put Him and His principles first in your life, He will show you His plan for you. He will put a thought in your mind that you never had before, or bring some concept to you that shows you how to turn your financial losses into financial gain.

God has a way of canceling out our debts and turning situations around. But you will never discover His plan until you seek Him first. As you follow God's roadmap, Matthew 6:33 wisely counsels, "Seek first His kingdom and His righteousness, and all these things will be added to you."

It's a promise—a promise you can take all the way to the bank.

NOTES

CHAPTER 3: VICTORY

1. Money 101, Lesson 9: Controlling Debt. Online article, CNN Money website, http://money.cnn.com/magazines/moneymag/money101/lesson9/index.htm
2. Quote from Randy Alcorn taken from a sermon based on the author's book *The Treasure Principle* that he shared at a Crown Financial Ministries pastors' conference a few years ago.
3. The Barna Group, "The Economy's Impact (part 3 of 3): Donors Reduce Giving, Brace for the Long Haul," http://www.barna.org/barna-update/article/18-congregations/341-the-economys-impact-part-3-of-3-donors-reduce-giving-brace-for-the-long-haul?q=tithe
4. James Strong, *Strong's Exhaustive Concordance of the Bible with Greek and Hebrew Dictionaries*, #H4643.

THE URBAN
ALTERNATIVE

D r. Tony Evans and The Urban Alternative (TUA) equips, **empowers**, and **unites** Christians to **impact** *individuals, families, churches,* and *communities* to restore hope and transform lives.

We believe the core cause of the problems we face in our personal lives, homes, churches, and societies is a spiritual one; therefore, the only way to address them is spiritually. We've tried a political, a social, an economic, and even a religious agenda. It's time for a Kingdom Agenda—God's visible and comprehensive rule over every area of life because when we function as we were designed, there is a divine power that changes everything. It renews and restores as the life of Christ is made manifest within our own. As we align ourselves under Him, there is an alignment that happens from deep within—where He brings about full restoration. It is an atmosphere that revives and makes whole.

As it impacts us, it impacts others—transforming every sphere of life in which we live. When each biblical sphere of life functions in accordance with God's Word, the outcomes are evangelism, discipleship, and community impact. As we learn how to govern ourselves under God, we then transform the institutions of family, church, and society from a biblically based kingdom perspective. Through Him, we are touching heaven and changing earth.

To achieve our goal, we use a variety of strategies, methods, and resources for reaching and equipping as many people as possible.

BROADCAST MEDIA

Hundreds of thousands of individuals experience *The Alternative with Dr. Tony Evans* through the daily radio broadcast playing on more than **850 radio outlets** and in more than **80 countries**. The broadcast can also be seen on several television networks and is viewable online at TonyEvans.org.

LEADERSHIP TRAINING

The Kingdom Agenda Pastors (KAP) provides a *viable network* for *like-minded pastors* who embrace the Kingdom

Agenda philosophy. Pastors have the opportunity to go deeper with Dr. Tony Evans as they are given greater biblical knowledge, practical applications, and resources to impact individuals, families, churches, and communities. KAP welcomes senior and associate pastors of all churches.

The Kingdom Agenda Pastors' Summit progressively develops church leaders to meet the demands of the 21st century while maintaining the gospel message and the strategic position of the church. The Summit introduces *intensive seminars, workshops,* and *resources,* addressing issues affecting the community, family, leadership, organizational health, and more.

Pastors' Wives Ministry, founded by Dr. Lois Evans, provides *counsel, encouragement,* and *spiritual resources* for pastors' wives as they serve with their husbands in the ministry. A primary focus of the ministry is the KAP Summit that offers senior pastors' wives a safe place to *reflect, renew,* and *relax* along with training in personal development, spiritual growth, and care for their emotional and physical well-being.

COMMUNITY IMPACT

National Church Adopt-A-School Initiative (NCAASI) prepares churches across the country to impact communities by using *public schools as the primary vehicle for effecting positive social change* in urban youth and families. Leaders of churches, school districts, faith-based organizations, and other nonprofit organizations are equipped with the knowledge and tools to *forge partnerships* and build *strong social service delivery systems.*

This training is based on the comprehensive church-based community impact strategy conducted by Oak Cliff Bible Fellowship. It addresses such areas as economic development, education, housing, health revitalization, family renewal, and racial reconciliation. We also assist churches in tailoring the model to meet the specific needs of their communities while simultaneously addressing the spiritual and moral frame of reference.

RESOURCE DEVELOPMENT

We are fostering lifelong learning partnerships with the people we serve by providing a variety of published materials. We offer booklets, Bible studies, books, CDs, and DVDs to strengthen people in their walk with God and ministry to others.

* * *

For more information, a catalog of Dr. Tony Evans'
ministry resources, and a complimentary copy of
Dr. Evans' devotional newsletter,
call (800) 800-3222
or write TUA at P.O. Box 4000, Dallas TX 75208,
or log on to
TonyEvans.org

FOR MARRIED MEN ONLY

FOR MARRIED WOMEN ONLY

ISBN-13: 978-0-802... ...3-0

ISBN-13: 978-0-8024-4382-3

How is a wife to love her husband? By learning three things, says Tony Evans: how to submit, seduce, and surrender to her husband. Out of these three principles a godly marriage willgrow. Straight-forward yet encouraging.

What does It mean for a husband to love his wife? Three things, says Tony Evans: a husband must be his wife's savior, sanctifier, and satisfier. It is by living out these three principles that a godly marriage will blossom and flourish.

MOODY
PUBLISHERS
moodypublishers.com

MARRIAGE MATTERS

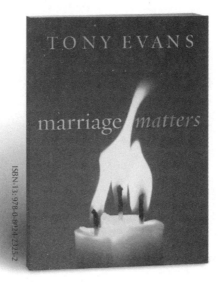

ISBN-13: 978-0-8024-2325-2

Marriage Matters examines the nature of the covenant, or agreement, we enter into on our wedding day. This booklet provides the foundation for the booklets *For Married Women Only* and *For Married Men Only*, as Evans looks to the Scriptures to define what a covenant is, who makes it, and what the implications are. Let the practical and engaging Tony Evans lead you in knowing just how much...Marriage Matters.

MOODY
PUBLISHERS
moodypublishers.com